A PASTORAL COUNSELING
GUIDEBOOK

CHARLES F. KEMP

NASHVILLE ABINGDON PRESS NEW YORK

A PASTORAL COUNSELING GUIDEBOOK

Copyright © 1971 by Abingdon Press

ISBN 0-687-30320-6

PRINTED AND BOUND BY THE
PARTHENON PRESS, AT NASHVILLE,
TENNESSEE, UNITED STATES OF AMERICA

Acknowledgments

Many people have contributed to the completion of this material. My colleagues in the Pastoral Care and Training Center, Dr. Robert Glen, our psychiatric consultant, Dr. Marcus Bryant of Brite Divinity School, and Mr. Charles Sanders, director of the Center, have read the material in its entirety and made many helpful suggestions. Dr. C. W. Brister of Southwestern Baptist Theological Seminary has been serving as a consultant and supervisor with us, and has also read the entire manuscript. Dr. E. Mansell Pattison, professor of psychiatry at the University of Washington, read it in its early stages and offered helpful suggestions. Several groups of advanced students who served on the staff of the Center as pastoral counselors have used it as the basis of many group discussions. Mrs. Jane Brabb, receptionist of the Pastoral Care and Training Center, and Miss Ginger Brittain spent many hours typing the material, and their help is sincerely appreciated also.

Preface

The outlines of topics on pastoral counseling were first prepared as a basis for discussions by the counseling and supervisory staff of the Pastoral Care and Training Center of Brite Divinity School, Texas Christian University. (For a description of this Center and its principles of operation see Appendix I.) Their purpose was very practical and often specific. It was to help those who were doing extensive pastoral counseling to clarify their thinking and increase their understanding of the task.

Each topic was originally a "Memo" to be read by the individual and then used as the basis of a discussion at a weekly seminar. The topics were first presented in loose-leaf form to be placed in a notebook so that each one serving on the staff could add his own conclusions from the discussion, or from his reading, his observation, or his experience.

Three different groups of counselors, all postgraduate theological students, used them over a two-year period in this way. In addition they have been used as the basis for discussion in several pastors' conferences, and a number of pastors have purchased them in notebook form as a basis for individual study. It is in response to these experiences that we have been led to prepare this material for wider circulation.

We have reworked the material, deleted those references to a specific situation, and made the topics applicable either to a local parish or a pastoral counseling center.

In its original form it was a handbook prepared for use by a specific group. In its present form it is a guidebook. It is designed to provide several services, and to be used in a variety of ways.

1. Much has been done to further an understanding of counseling procedures and the therapeutic relationship in recent years. Much of this information has been condensed with the outlines that form the main body of this guidebook. These can be read straight through as one would read any book, to secure the information.

2. The material was prepared to form the basis of a notebook in which a person would gather his own information. Suggestions for further study have been included throughout the material. These outlines have intentionally been kept brief and concise. Illustrations and extensive quotations have been excluded. The purpose was to provide an outline which each pastor could expand, and to which he could add illustrations from his own experience and quotations from his own reading. Then his study of the material would become both practical and creative.

3. The outlines could be the basis of group discussion as well as individual study. Our ideas really become our own when we have to defend them, clarify them, or explain them to others. Students in schools, pastors in a community, and students in a clinical pastoral education center could use these outlines as the basis of discussion.

4. Reading and discussion have value only when they are related to actual experience. Throughout the body of the material, suggestions for relating theory to practice are included. These also could be the basis of either group discussion or individual study.

5. The material also has been prepared so that it can serve as a handbook of community resources and pastoral aid materials. Blanks have been included so that a person can include the names, addresses, and phone numbers of those individuals and agencies that might be consulted and referred to, as well as the titles of more books and pamphlets that might be utilized. In this way it can become a handy reference for all practical tasks.

6. One of the real by-products of working with others is that one grows himself in the process. Indeed, the pastor should be in a process of constant growth and understanding. Suggestions of how this material may be utilized for personal growth are also included.

One or more of these suggestions for continued use of the Guidebook are included after each outline. The extent to which one uses these projects is, of course, optional. The more they are used, the more growth will take place.

We are well aware that many other topics could be included in this Guidebook. There are limits of space. We are also conscious that these topics are not all-inclusive. They weren't meant to be. It is a Guidebook which hopefully will lead to further study. We do not pretend that all areas discussed are of equal importance. That would, of course, be ridiculous. Some very brief statements may have more significance than others that are of greater length. We do feel that all topics that are included have practical application and that all are of real importance. We further feel that the pastor's task is one of the most needed and profoundly relevant tasks in the world today and that any tool that helps him perform it more effectively is needed.

This manual should be used in conjunction with an earlier workbook, Learning About Pastoral Care, published by Abingdon Press in 1970, which covers the broad sweep of pastoral care. If one works through the exercises in it, and studies and expands the outlines here, he should have a good background in the fundamentals of pastoral counseling and pastoral care.

Contents

The Pastoral Counselor and His People

The world is full of troubled persons. They exist in far greater numbers than most people realize. They are present in every city, every community, every congregation. Many are not recognized as being troubled at all because they hide their hurt, their loneliness, their guilt behind a facade of activity, conversation, work, and pleasure. But the hurt is there nonetheless.

Many of these people seek the help of a pastor. There is no experience in the ministry that presents a man with a greater opportunity or a deeper responsibility than when some troubled person seeks his help. When he plans a program or preaches a sermon, he hopes he is meeting real and important needs. If he knows his people, he probably is. On the occasions when he sits down with someone troubled with doubt, anxiety, or guilt, when he tries to help someone make an important decision or resolve a problem, he knows he is dealing with a real issue. In a very real sense, destiny is in his hands. He has no more sacred responsibility than this.

The number of dynamics that takes place when two people meet to discuss a life situation is almost unbelievable.

First, there is the pastor himself and all that he brings to the conversation. What he can contribute to the situation is influenced by all his background, his experience, his training, his skill, his knowledge, his attitudes, his personality traits, his goals for counseling, and his personal adjustment. All these things are important. (See Section 2, "The Pastor's Attitudes," and Section 1, "Goals of Pastoral Counseling.")

THE PASTOR AND WHAT HE BRINGS TO COUNSELING

His own experience
His training
His skills
His attitudes toward people
His goals in counseling
His personality traits
His own adjustments
His faith and commitment

Pastor

The parishioner or counselee also brings a whole complex combination of factors to the experience. There is the immediate problem that is causing him concern. There are other problems of which he may not even be aware. There is his entire background, his childhood, his homelife, his educational and vocational experience, his attitudes toward the clergy, his expectations of counseling, his own self-image--which is usually low--(See Section 4, "Considerations in a Counselor's First Interview"), his resources both personal and spiritual, his limitations, and his strengths. (See Section 12, "Building on Strengths.") All have an influence on what takes place, what will be accomplished, and what growth can be attained.

WHAT THE PARISHIONER BRINGS TO COUNSELING

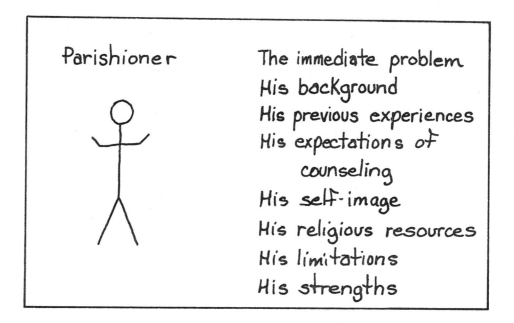

The two persons meet and a new relationship is formed.

The pastor's first and one of his foremost responsibilities is to establish the kind of relationship that is healing, strengthening, honest, challenging, and productive of growth. (See Section 3, "The Pastoral Counseling Relationship.") It is a confidential relationship based on mutual trust. (See Section 31, "Confidential Information and Privileged Communication.") It is characterized by certain key words, such as empathy, rapport, understanding. Unfortunately, they can become trite or superficial. Rightfully understood they are at the heart of the counseling process. Basically they embody traditional Christian compassion and love, combined with psychological understanding. Both are important.

THE COUNSELING RELATIONSHIP

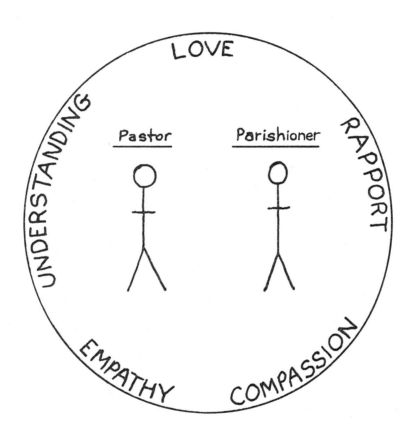

At the same time that he is establishing a relationship the pastor is also evaluating the situation. Some people object to the term "diagnosis" because it is a medical term, but that is basically what he is doing. He is exploring many questions: What is the real need here? What lies behind the problem? Is it in my area of competence? Is this something someone else could do better? What can be done immediately? What are the long-range goals, etc.? To do this he uses all the resources at his disposal. He listens (see Section 5). He is aware of nonverbal clues (see Section 6), and he uses tests when indicated, or suggests that they be administered (see Section 7, "Mental and Psychological Tests" and Section 8, "Evaluating Intelligence"). He uses any means that will help him understand a person. (See Section 10, "Assessment of Personality.") He knows this person is under stress (see Section 11), so he proceeds accordingly. He keeps all diagnosis and evaluations temporary, for he knows that new information and further discussion may present quite new and different material. (See Section 9, "Evaluation and Diagnosis.")

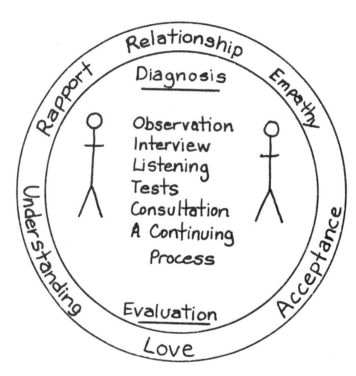

Relationship
Rapport
Diagnosis
Empathy

Observation
Interview
Listening
Tests
Consultation
A Continuing
Process

Understanding
Evaluation
Acceptance
Love

After he has made his initial evaluation, the pastor may determine that this is not something that he should attempt personally. In most cases he will retain his relationship as a pastor, but he may turn to the community for help. There may be people who have training, skill, resources, equipment, and time that he does not have. (See Section 25, "Principles of Referral"; Section 27, "Psychiatric Referral"; Section 28, "The Counselor and the Physician"; and Section 30, "Concerning Legal Matters.") The pastor must know both the principles of referral and the community agencies. (See Section 26, "Information About an Agency," and Appendix 6, "Referral Resources.") This information in itself can provide a great service, since people are often unaware of the resources that are available.

Referral may be of several kinds. It may be for complete care, the pastor continuing as pastor, but with a psychiatrist or some other agency assuming responsibility for the counseling. There may be a situation where the pastor refers one member of a family and he continues with the other. Or referral may be for a special service, such as testing, speech therapy, or vocational placement, with the pastor continuing with the counseling. It may be referral for consultation services where a specialist makes an evaluation and then consults with the pastor to help him minister more effectively.

MINISTRY OF REFERRAL

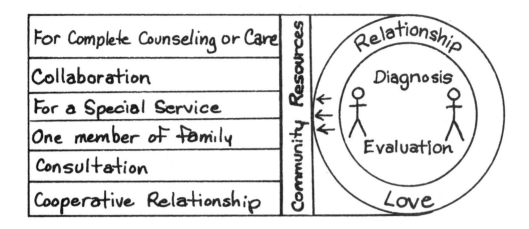

For Complete Counseling or Care	
Collaboration	
For a Special Service	
One member of family	
Consultation	
Cooperative Relationship	

It may be that after the pastor has made his initial evaluation he feels there is an area in which he as a pastor can be of help. The pastor feels that the person, or persons, will respond to pastoral counseling. (See Section 13, "Pastoral Counseling Techniques.") Then the question remains to be answered, what procedures, or methods will be of the greatest help? Here the pastor is indebted to the many developments that have taken place in the fields of counseling, guidance, and psychotherapy, and to the development of pastoral counseling. As a pastor he draws on resources wherever they are available. His one concern is for the welfare of his people. To help them he uses what he can. He may feel that what one person needs most is support, reassurance, a knowledge that someone is standing by. Because of his symbolic role the pastor has a unique contribution to offer here. (See Section 15, "Supportive Counseling.") He may feel that the person is confused, that he needs more understanding, and that insight counseling is what is indicated. In this case, he would utilize "reflection of feelings" as advocated by Carl Rogers and the client-centered approach, or interpretation as Adler might explain one's life-style. (See Section 16, "Insight Counseling.") He may feel that the person's behavior is a result of conditioning, and he may utilize the findings of learning theory or behavior modification (see Section 17, "Application of Behavior Modification to Pastoral Counseling"), particularly reenforcement and extinction. Any such procedure should be used only when the pastor has had some training and preferably some supervision in its use.

It may be that the person lacks purpose or meaning, and the pastor may draw upon the thought of Viktor Frankl or the existential therapist (see Section 18, "The Search for Meaning").

The pastor may feel that the problem is basically a guidance problem; that the person lacks sufficient or adequate information or needs to develop new skills, make decisions, etc. If so, then he might well use the guidance approach. (See Section 19, "Guidance and Pastoral Care"; Section 20, "Educational Guidance and Academic Problems; Section 21 "Premarital Counseling and Guidance.")

Other emphases may be included, such as Glasser's Reality Therapy and the demand for responsibility, Berne's PAC, or Mowrer's Integrity Therapy, etc. (See Section 14, "Techniques Used by Schools of Psychotherapy.")

There will be numerous occasions when a person does not come alone. The majority of problems that are brought to a pastor or taken to a pastoral counseling center are family problems. In these instances the pastor establishes a relationship not with one person, but with two--

16

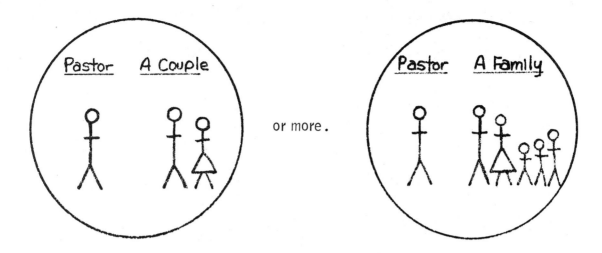

or more.

Sometimes it is with a couple anticipating marriage; at other times, with people who are having difficulty in their home. (See Section 21, "Premarital Counseling and Guidance;" Section 22, "Family Counseling;" and Section 23, "Filial Therapy.")

Since he is a pastor, he makes a unique contribution that no other counselor can make in quite the same way. He has a symbolic role which can create some problems, but can also be used as a source of strength. (See Section 55, "What Is Unique About Pastoral Counseling.") He has had specialized training which enables him to see man from a theological or religious standpoint. (See Sect. 53, "The Nature of Man.") He can utilize the healing, strengthening forces of religious worship, both public and private. (See Sect. 40, "Utilizing the Public Worship Service," and Sect. 41, "The Use of Personal Religious Worship as an Adjunct to Counseling Sessions.") He can teach people the great truths of the Christian faith, instruct them in the devotional life, and help them gain an understanding of religious values and the nature of religious experience. (See Sect. 38, "The Teaching Function of Pastoral Counseling.") He can relate people to a redemptive fellowship, the church. He can challenge them to acts of service, which can be strengthening and therapeutic. He can challenge people to Christian commitment and assure them of divine grace and forgiveness. (See Sect. 39, "Religious Resources," Sect. 42, "Guilt, Confession, and Forgiveness," and Sect. 43, "Conversion".)

The pastor does not feel that he is dependent on his own wisdom or his own skill. He feels and can help the parishioner (counselee) to feel that God is also concerned and present in the counseling process. (See Sect. 54, "The Holy Spirit in Pastoral Counseling," and Sect. 39, "Religious Resources".) This is a great source of strength.

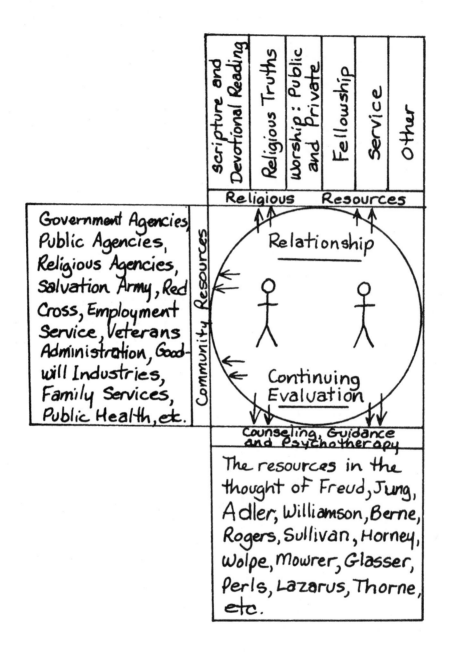

It may be that in addition to his own counseling, or the use of the community, or the resources of the church, the pastor feels that there are other things the person could be doing that would relieve tension, foster growth, and increase his understanding. (See Sect. 44, "Adjuncts to Counseling.") These may include the use of reading material that will broaden his perspective or provide inspiration or information about the family, religious faith, or life in general. (See Sect. 45,

"Bibliotherapy.") It may be that the time between sessions can be used in ways that will increase insight and self-understanding. (See Sect. 46, "Free Writing.") Many things can be done to supplement what is done in the counseling hour. If a person can just be helped to develop a hobby or learn to relax or take regular physical exercises, he may relieve much of his tension. (See Sect. 14, "Techniques Used by Schools of Psychotherapy.") The point is that all the resources that are available should be utilized.

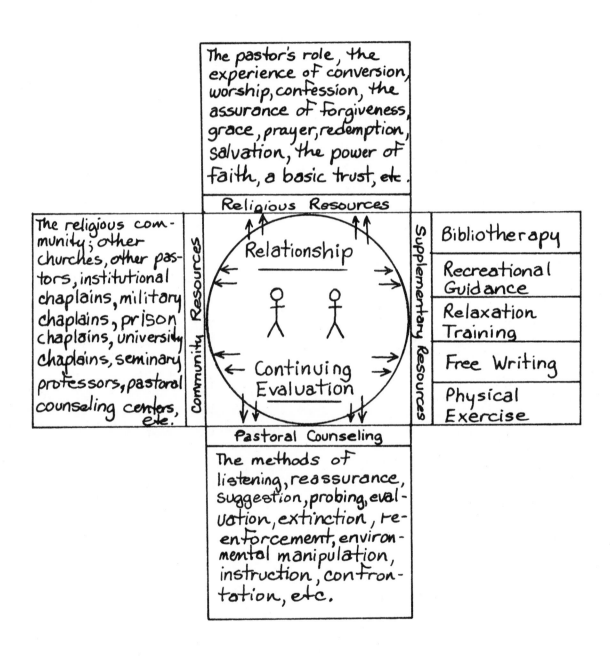

A pastor, of necessity, is a general practitioner. He deals with all kinds of people. Some with whom he counsels are old, some are young. (See Sect. 24, "Counseling with Adolescents.") Some are wise, some are simple. (See Sect. 8, "Evaluating Intelligence.") Some are wealthy, some may be in poverty. (See Sect. 47, "Counseling the Poor and Disadvantaged.") Some may need practical, material help. They may need money, food, clothing, or a job. (See Sect. 48, "Material Aid and Practical Assistance.") Some will come willingly, anxious and ready to cooperate, some come hesitantly--even angrily. (See Sect. 33, "Those Who Come to the Pastor Unwillingly.")

Some can be helped immediately, quickly. Some may take a long time and require extended or continuous counseling. (See Sect. 35, "The Middle Phases of Extended Counseling," and Sect. 36, "Termination of Counseling.") With some the counseling progresses easily and smoothly. With others, it is characterized by setbacks and resistance, and in spite of the pastor's best efforts little progress seems to take place. (See Sect. 32, "Some Problems in Counseling.") With some persons, it is hard to establish communication. The pastor does not understand the counselee, and the counselee may not understand the pastor. This is particularly true if there is a cultural, racial, or generation gap. (See Sect. 34, "Semantics and Communication".)

At times, the counseling relationship may be very puzzling and confusing. The attitudes of understanding and acceptance the pastor intended to establish may be difficult to maintain. The parishioner (counselee) may seem to resent his efforts, even to oppose them. Instead of love, the pastor is greeted with hostility. At other times the counselee may respond with a show of appreciation or even affection that may be embarrassing. Such feelings must be recognized and understood. (See Sect. 37, "Transference and Countertransference.")

All this can be very time-consuming. It often seems that the pastor is spending an inordinate amount of time for what is being accomplished. Actually this is not true.

Let us assume that the pastor sees the parishioner for one hour once a week for a month. Let one circle ◯ represent one rotation of the clock, or twelve hours. A day, or twenty-four hours would be represented by two circles, one above ⑧ ¹ the other. If the pastor sees the parishioner for one hour once a week, ⑧ hour from 3:00 to 4:00 p.m. on Monday, that counseling hour would be filled in. Thus, using these symbols, we can clearly show the proportion of time spent in counseling to the total number of hours in a day--or a week or a month. One week would look like this:

MON. TUES. WED. THURS. FRI. SAT. SUN.   1 hour of coun-
⑧   8   8   8   8   8   8   seling, 167 other
                                        hours in 1 week.

20

A month would add 3 more weeks

8 8 8 8 8 8 8   2 hours coun-
                seling, 334 other
                hours in 2 weeks.

8 8 8 8 8 8 8   3 hours coun-
                seling, 501 other
                hours in 3 weeks.

8 8 8 8 8 8 8   4 hours counseling,
                768 other hours
                in 1 month.

Four hours to counteract one's entire life before, against 768 hours of other environmental influences is really not a great deal of time.

Not all the pastor's counseling will be done in his own office. On occasion he will go to the hospital, where he may also be presented with a counseling situation. (See Sect. 29, "Pastoral Counseling in the Hospital.") Not all the people can come to the pastor. Some he will need to visit in their homes or in a nursing home or home for older people. (See Sect. 49, "Pastoral Care of Shut-ins.")

Counseling is no easy task. At times it can be very tiring, frustrating, and discouraging. The sensitive pastor will be well aware of his own limitations and weaknesses. If he is sincere in his desire to serve his people, he will engage in a constant program of self-improvement. The outlines presented here could well be a means for an individual's continued study and growth. A group of pastors could use them as a guide for group discussion also.

There are many publications that could be consulted for further understanding (see Bibliography). Many men have recorded the fruits of their experience to help others serve more effectively.

One of the most effective means of growth is to keep a record of one's own counseling experiences and study the results. (See Section 50 "Keeping Records.") One can also study and evaluate his own attitudes and counseling techniques (see Appendix 7, "Checklist of Pastoral Attitudes" and also Appendix 8, "Checklist of Counseling Principles and Procedures"). It is even better if a pastor can receive the services of a psychiatrist, psychologist, social worker, or specialist in pastoral care to go over the records and procedures with him.

The rewards a pastor receives for such efforts will not be monetary and may go unnoticed, but they will be very real. Some people will want to pay for his services, and some probably should. At least they should contribute to the church or agency that makes his services possible (see Section 51, "The Problem of Fees"). In spite of the discouragement and the frustration in his job the pastor will see real growth take place in people's lives, and this is reward enough. He will also see growth in his own life. Whatever the results he serves faithfully and well. He knows he is not called to be successful--not even as a counselor. He is called to be faithful, a faithful servant. As such he does his best. (See Section 52, "Toward a Code of Ethics.") Each time he helps another he becomes stronger and more understanding. As his effectiveness increases, the service he can render becomes larger and he has the inner satisfaction of knowing he has fulfilled the wishes of One who said, "As you did it to one of the least of these my brethren, you did it to me" (Matt. 25:40).

Outlines of Pastoral Counseling Principles and Procedures

1. THE GOALS OF PASTORAL COUNSELING

Any effective counseling depends upon the counselor's having certain clearly defined goals and objectives. The goals and objectives will differ with the institution in which a person works and the area of specialization he chooses. The following are goals of the pastor whether he is serving a local church or is on the staff of a pastoral counseling center. They are not attained all at once. All of them are not attempted in one interview. Not all of them may be needed by any one counselee; yet, in the main, these are the things a pastor hopes to do.

1. Reduce undue tension. Most counselees, perhaps all, have some tension, and some should have. One purpose of the pastor is to help counselees drain off their emotion and reduce their anxiety. This in itself is a real service and may be all that some people need.

2. Resolve harmful conflicts. Many people who come to the pastor are involved in conflict with spouse, children, parents, professors, employers, etc. Hostility, when it is uncontrolled, can destroy. Controlled anger can be positive in its results because understanding and love build.

3. Improve insight and self-understanding. Insight is more than a knowledge about oneself. It is an emotional understanding that enables one to understand his feelings and his tensions. Anything that promotes self-understanding is helpful to the counselee. There are occasions when insight is too threatening, or when it may lead to action that is inappropriate.

4. Increase self-acceptance. Most counselees have a poor self-image. They find it difficult to accept themselves as they are. Acceptance comes not by persuasion but by our acceptance of them and through their deeper understanding of their own needs and problems.

5. Release internal resources. Most people have within themselves resources of strength, which can be drawn upon. At times these need to be identified. At times a bit of encouragement, support, or reassurance will enable them to master their own ego strengths and cope with their own problems.

6. Provide information. Often the information that people have is limited, faulty, or confused by emotion. Some problems cannot be solved without clarifying confusion; some decisions cannot be reached without adequate information. At times the counselor is a "friendly teacher."

7. Foster continued growth. Not only must their immediate problems be solved and their immediate decisions be made, but persons must also grow in the process, they must attain new levels of behavior. That which fosters continued growth is the identification of rewards in the immediate situation.

8. Make realistic choices. Some persons come to the pastor facing decisions about marriage, education, or careers. People need to be helped to make intelligent choices and realistic plans toward their realization, if these are possible.

9. Improve interpersonal relationships. A basic purpose of all pastoral work is to help people understand and accept each other--in other words, to help persons love and be loved.

10. Attain self-fulfillment and self-actualization. Pastoral counseling is concerned not only with resolving conflicts, but with movement towards attaining one's potential, and the realization of meaning and purpose.

11. Deepen spiritual resources. People need to discover spiritual resources, to deepen their understanding of spiritual resources, and to live lives of faith. This is not easy; it varies with the person's background and with the counselor's own experience, but it is the ultimate goal of pastoral counseling.

RELATING THEORY TO PRACTICE: It is important that each person think through his own individual goals and objectives that will guide and motivate his work.

1. Write out your own goals for your pastoral counseling without consulting this list, stating them in your own words. Then compare with this list.

2. Read the entire text of this Guidebook. Then write out your list again. Whether you agree with this list is not important. You may combine, delete, expand, or add to as you prefer. What is important is that you have clearly defined goals for your work, which are in a constant state of evaluation, revision, and improvement.

3. The above procedures can become a mere intellectual exercise unless they are related to actual situations. Take any counseling cases with which you are now working and write out what your goals are for that person (or persons). Ask yourself: What goals are realistic? What goals are possible? Consider what are the immediate goals, and what are the long-range goals. It will be helpful if you write them out. This does much to focus your attention and clarify your thinking as well as prevent abstract, unrelated thinking.

2. THE PASTOR'S ATTITUDES

While skills and techniques are important, one of the most influential factors in pastoral counseling is the attitude of the counselor. The following list is something of a checklist. No one has ever attained all the things on the list to perfection. On some days and with some persons, our attitudes are more positive than others. Actually, attitudes all overlap and combine to make up a person's total approach. The following list of attitudes may be used as a guide for self-evaluation and growth, and should be developed and maintained.

1. Concentration. Achievement in any important field demands intense concentration: athletics, scholarship, research, the arts. It is equally true of counseling. The counselee should feel and know that the counselor is giving him his undivided attention.

2. Understanding. No person fully understands another. We only understand in part, but it helps the counselee if he feels the counselor is making every effort to understand him.

3. Respect. We are using this in a religious sense. The pastoral counselor sees every man as a child of God and therefore worthy of his efforts and attention.

4. Acceptance. Every person must be accepted as a person of unconditional worth. This does not mean that evil is ignored or misbehavior condoned. It means that the pastoral counselor must accept the counselee in spite of his behavior, his opinions, or his beliefs. This acceptance must be sincere. If the person really feels accepted, he will be helped.

5. Objectivity. This does not mean aloofness, professionalism, or indifference. A pastoral counselor must be involved, related to the counselee in depth, but always objectively. This is one of his greatest services. A person cannot be objective about himself.

6. Patience. Counseling takes time. Progress is often slow. One outstanding pastor said, "There's something about the slow, hard task of changing life that few have the patience to endure." Actually, remarkable results do take place with a relatively small expenditure of time. It is easy not to recognize this and to become impatient. The pastor must be patient.

7. Confidence. The pastoral counselor must work with confidence. He must be confident of his methods. He must have confidence in the counseling process. This requires thorough, careful, and continued preparation and study.

8. Optimism. Optimism can be neither superficial nor sentimental. It must be genuine and sincere. The Christian faith affirms that prodigals can become sons again. Secular therapists begin a situation believing that growth, change, and understanding can take place. The pastoral counselor can do no less. The counselees have little confidence and are often pessimistic and discouraged. The pastoral counselor must maintain hope.

9. Love. Again we would stress that this cannot be superficial and sentimental; it must be objective and realistic. The pastoral counselor must care; he must care enough to become involved; he must care enough to be himself in the relationship with genuine concern and compassion.

10. Dedication. Frederick McKinney, in his book Counseling for Personal Adjustment,* says that a counselor's office should be a "sanctuary." A sanctuary by definition is a "holy" place. A worship room is called a sanctuary because sacred things take place there. Equally sacred things take place in a counseling room. People are making confession, facing decisions, looking at themselves, developing their potentiality, growing in understanding. Such matters can only be dealt with in a spirit of Christian commitment.

11. Faith. The pastoral counselor believes that God is more concerned about the counselee than the pastor is; therefore, he doesn't have to play God. He feels that God is present in the counseling situation though the word God may never be mentioned. It is because of his faith that the pastor can be patient and accepting and optimistic. In serving men he is in truth serving God, and therefore proceeds by faith.

*(Houghton-Mifflin, 1958).

FOR PERSONAL GROWTH: The development of attitudes is a lifetime task. Changes in attitudes usually come slowly over an extended period of time. The development of new attitudes requires strong motivation, much discipline, patience, persistence, and, at times, the assistance of others.

1. Reread the list suggested. Make any additions or changes you prefer. Rewrite the list in your own words.

2. Note any areas where you feel you need particular growth or change. Much can be done to develop and strengthen one's attitudes by making them the basis of meditation and worship. Any permanent growth requires a regular procedure over a period of time. One's pastoral work should be a part of whatever personal worship or prayer he observes. There is nothing more significant to concentrate upon than the pastor's own attitudes.

3. When one is aware that there are certain attitudes that are particularly negative—that may be affecting his counseling adversely—he might well seek counseling about them.

RELATING THEORY TO PRACTICE: This should not be merely introspective. One should relate it to actual counseling procedures. Reflect back on any recent counseling sessions. If records of such sessions have been kept it is even better. List the attitudes you felt, how they affected the feelings of the counselee, the outcome of the session, etc. For all current and future counseling sessions write out your attitudes, ask why you feel as you do, what changes need to be developed, etc.?

3. THE PASTORAL COUNSELING RELATIONSHIP

Frederick McKinney, in Counseling for Personal Adjustment, said, "Of all the factors that influence counseling, the interpersonal relationship is the most important."[*] Carl Rogers is speaking of the same thing when he says, "If we can provide a certain kind of relationship, growth and change will take place."[**] What is true of other counselors is equally true of pastoral counselors.

This relationship is referred to as "rapport." According to the dictionary this is a relationship between people characterized by "a close understanding or working in mutual dependence." Generally such a relationship is referred to as a "good" relationship. It cannot be overemphasized that when the relationship is good, good results usually occur. This may explain why pastors in previous generations were

[*]McKinney, p. 229.
[**]Rogers, On Becoming a Person (Houghton-Mifflin, 1961), p. 33.

often highly successful, even though they had no training in counseling and no technical knowledge of psychology. The relationship they had with their parishioners, which was characterized by understanding, compassion, and concern, did produce results.

To stress the importance of the relationship in no wise minimizes or depreciates the value or need of training in techniques or the dynamics of behavior.

On the contrary, it intensifies its importance. It is through understanding and techniques that a good relationship is established. By the very nature of the case the pastor must often work with people where the relationship is not good. He cannot select his parishioners as a psychotherapist selects his clients. By the proper use of techniques, and because of his understanding of what is taking place, the pastor can continue to be of help, even though the relationship may be strained, and in so doing, can often improve the relationship.

Certain factors about this relationship should be kept in mind:

1. It is an imperfect relationship. All interpersonal relationships are subject to strain and tension. Because of different backgrounds, different feelings, limits of time, and many other things, two people cannot always have the perfect accord, harmony, affinity they might wish. This does not mean that results cannot take place.

2. It is a changing relationship. It is never constant; it is subject to stresses and strains as any other relationship is. Sometimes all runs smoothly; at other times tension is present.

3. It is a professional relationship. The pastor by virtue of ordination, training, and position plays a particular role. The person or parishioner comes to him because he is a pastor. (See Section 1 dealing with pastoral goals.)

4. It is an emotional relationship. Matters of deep feeling are discussed. Great issues in a person's life are involved. Feelings are inevitable. The phenomenon of transference and counter transference should always be kept in mind. (See Section 37, "Transference and Counter Transference.)

5. It is an empathetic relationship. "Empathy" is the word that has replaced sympathy in counseling literature. It refers to the counselor's attempts to "enter into the inner frame of reference" of the person--to feel "with," not "sorry for." Empathy requires skill, training, imagination, concern, and objectivity.

6. It is a unique relationship, one in which two persons concentrate on the deepest concerns, hopes, fears, goals, doubts, and faith of each other. Nothing is excluded at the appropriate time. Guilt, resentment, hostility, hopes, and aspirations may all be considered. There is almost no other relationship in a person's life in which this takes place.

7. It is a purposeful or goal-seeking relationship. This is in contrast to such a relationship as friendship, for example, which exists for its own sake. In the counseling relationship two people concentrate on relieving stress, learning to live with reality, attempting to understand and solve a problem, improving behavior, or deepening the faith of one of them.

8. It is a mutual relationship. While the main goal is the resolving of the difficulty of the parishioner, both parties benefit, both become involved, both share

the responsibility according to their role and capacity, both learn, and both grow in the process.

9. It is an understanding relationship. This is always imperfect and subject to more knowledge and insight. The pastor makes every effort to try to understand. Even though his understanding is imperfect and incomplete, the knowledge that someone is trying to understand helps the counselee.

10. It is an accepting relationship. Acceptance is a key word in the literature of psychotherapy and theology. Carl Rogers said that the client must be accepted as a person of unconditional worth, and Paul Tillich said, "Though we are unacceptable we are still accepted." Acceptance is also a deceiving word. Many confuse it with condoning. Accepting a person does not mean condoning his behavior. Beginning counselors often assume that accepting a person is easy. The truth is that it is very difficult, because it involves accepting persons who resist us as well as those who cooperate with us. It means accepting persons whose behavior, ideas, and ideals differ from our own. To do this takes discipline, training, practice, and understanding. Acceptance can be an extremely powerful force, for many counselees have not experienced acceptance anyplace else.

11. It is a Christian relationship. It is based on love in the New Testament sense. Love that is "patient and kind . . . not jealous or boastful . . . not arrogant or rude. Love (that) does not insist on its own way; . . . is not irritable or resentful; . . . does not rejoice at wrong, but rejoices in the right. Love (that) bears all things, believes all things, hopes all things, endures all things" (I Cor. 13:4-7). The pastor finds his motive power, his inspiration, from the example and spirit of Christ. In the love, the compassion, the understanding, the patience, the faith that He demonstrated and revealed is the pastor's ultimate hope. No one follows Christ's example perfectly; in fact, we can only approach it from afar. We can move in the direction of a truly Christian relationship, and the degree to which we attain it will, to a large extent, determine the help we are able to provide.

RELATING THEORY TO PRACTICE: Review any recent counseling experiences and write out the things that seemed to characterize the relationship. Which of the items mentioned above were present? Were there other factors not included here? How did the relationship influence the outcome of the counseling? How could the relationship have been improved?

Do the same with all current and future counseling. Consider how the relationship changes from one session to another.

4. A COUNSELEE'S FIRST INTERVIEW

Every meaningful experience is accompanied by a mixture of emotions. Every new experience has elements of uncertainty and threat. Every attempt at self-understanding, growth, or self-evaluation has a combination of hope and fear, anxiety and anticipation.

When a person goes to a pastor or a counseling center, he goes out of a sense of need. For him the visit is a very meaningful experience. It is a new experience. He is in a strange environment. He does not know what to expect. In most cases this is his first experience at counseling.

His feelings are very mixed, often confused, and sometimes intense. He undoubtedly is anxious or he would not have come. He may be uncertain as to whether he is doing the right thing. He may be angry because someone has insisted that he come, or just because it is necessary that he come. He may be embarrassed that it seems necessary to seek help. He may feel guilty and ashamed of what he has done. He may be defensive about the fact that he has to talk about himself. He may be hesitant about the whole procedure. He may be resentful that he has to relate to an authority figure. He may be doubtful about the value of such an attempt. He may be suspicious that he will not be treated fairly or that the conversation may not be confidential. He may be hopeful that he will receive help. He may be confident now that he has made definite efforts to receive help.

Every person who goes to a pastor has some of the feelings that are underlined in the paragraph above, maybe a few more. The pastor should be very much aware of the inevitability of such emotions when he meets a person for the first time in a counseling relationship. The following suggestions should be kept in mind for the initial interview.

1. Because of the possibility that some of the emotions mentioned above may be present, every effort should be made to help the person be comfortable and relaxed.

2. Since the counselee probably does not understand what counseling involves, you should explain to him the procedures that will follow and what he can expect. He should know that there is no magic involved. He should realize that while the pastor may make suggestions, the ultimate decisions are always his. It is a problem-solving process, in which he must do most of the work. There are no ready-made solutions. Counseling is time-consuming, but the time is well spent. If professional helpers other than the pastor are needed, the counselee will be informed of that. He should be reassured that the relationship is confidential and that the procedures do produce results. Such explanations may come at the beginning of the counseling hour or at the end, depending on circumstances. They may be interjected one at a time as questions arise.

3. Make every effort to establish rapport with the person. This is done by being sincere--by exhibiting acceptance and understanding; by answering questions honestly and creating the emotional climate of integrity and trust.

4. Listen to the person's story. Give every opportunity for him to verbalize his concern and express his feelings. This is especially important in the initial interview. (Section 5 will deal with "Listening.")

5. Secure the information you need to help you understand the person and his problems, and to decide on your own course of action. This can be done by careful but cautious questioning. He should not feel he is being cross-examined or pushed too far.

6. Make a tentative evaluation or diagnosis of the person's need and problems. This is, of course, subject to change as more data is presented. However, it is important that one begin to develop some concept of the needs and dynamics involved.

7. Make a tentative estimate of the person's strengths and weaknesses, his capacity for insight, and his motivation for change.

8. Make a tentative decision as to the best course of counseling, whether support, guidance, insight, or some other procedure is indicated. This too may change with further discussions.

9. Make a tentative decision as to whether or not this person will need referral to someone else for special services, such as further psychological testing, medical treatment, etc.

10. Be sure that all practical arrangements are clear, so that the person knows if and when he is to return, what the time limits are, etc.

11. Give some assurance whenever possible. It may be helpful to commend a person because he came for help. Some feel that seeking help is a sign of weakness. Actually, it may be an indication of maturity and a sign of strength. Give the counselee the feeling that something has been accomplished, that a process has been started that can produce positive results.

There are also some things one should not do during the initial interview.

Do not argue or become involved in a debate with the person. This may be possible later on, but not now.

Do not probe too fast or ask too-personal questions. This can arouse resistance. There is time to secure such information when confidence and trust have been established.

Do not give a person an all-conclusive diagnosis or evaluation. Until all the story is told, you do not know what the problem may be.

Do not offer false promises or cheap reassurance, promise results in a brief period of time, or otherwise oversimplify the situation.

RELATING THEORY TO PRACTICE: After each initial interview write out what the counselee's feelings were, what was accomplished, what your initial evaluation of the situation was, and what your goals are for continuing sessions.

5. LISTENING

One thing a pastor can do, in almost every interview, that often is of great value is to listen. Give every counselee an opportunity to express himself fully, especially during the initial interview. Most will want to talk. Occasionally a shy, uncooperative, or resistant counselee may require other methods but, in many cases, you can spend most of the time in the initial interview and much of the time in other interviews just listening. There are some situations in which this is all that is needed. Consider the following quotations:

"The very small verbal part the counselor plays . . . might mislead him into thinking that he is not doing enough for the client. This would be a grave mistake. The counselor can do nothing more productive of therapy in the early interviews than to sit quietly and listen with sympathy and interest during these long releases."*

"Just the process of talking things over brings new clarity of insight, release from over-tension and a new objectivity."**

"If I can listen to what he can tell me, if I can understand how it seems to him, if I can see its personal meaning for him, if I can sense the emotional flavor which it has for him, then I will be releasing potent forces of change in him.***

"Strangely enough, not to say anything may at times have as much effect as using words."****

Listening, however, is not easy or simple. It takes effort, discipline, and training.

"What are the basic requirements as to the personality of the psychiatrist? If I were asked to answer this question in one sentence, I would reply, The psychotherapist must be able to listen. . . . This is an art few are able to practice without special training."*****

"All things and all men, so to speak, call on us with small or loud voices. They want us to listen, they want us to understand."******

The following statements stress some of the values of listening:
1. Only as the pastor listens can he know what the problem is and how the person feels.
2. It is through listening that the pastor establishes a relationship and develops rapport.
3. It is when he listens that he releases emotion, and reduces tension and helps a person gain insight.

*Quoted in Readings in Modern Methods of Counseling, ed. Arthur H. Brayfield, (Appleton-Century, 1950), p. 298.
**Milton E. Hahn and Malcolm S. MacLean, General Clinical Counseling (McGraw-Hill, 1950), p. 115.
***Rogers, On Becoming a Person, p. 332.
****Francis P. Robinson, Principles and Procedures in Student Counseling (Harper, 1950), p. 84.
*****Frieda Fromm-Reichmann, Principles of Psychotherapy.
******Paul Tillich, Love, Power, and Justice (Oxford University Press, 1954; Galaxy Books, 1960), p. 84.

4. While recognizing the value of listening, we also recognize that it has limitations and some dangers.

      a. A person can only handle so much anxiety at a time. On occasion it is best to restrain his free expression.

      b. There are times when it is necessary to ask questions and to direct the conversation.

5. Listening is not easy. It should not be confused with passivity. Listening requires complete concentration, involvement, and concern, and as such can be very helpful.

RELATING THEORY TO PRACTICE: If it is possible to tape some of your counseling sessions, play them back and keep a record of how much time you spent talking and how much listening. If taping is not possible, reflect honestly on what occurred, with the same questions in mind.

6. NONVERBAL CLUES TO UNDERSTANDING A COUNSELEE

Many things provide clues to the needs and feelings of a counselee. This includes, of course, his stated purpose which usually includes his feelings. Some nonverbal clues can substantiate, emphasize, or correct his stated feelings. None of the following should be considered definitive in and of themselves, but all are when evaluated with other things, such as the interview, tests, etc.

1. Physical symptoms which may be observed by the counselor or mentioned by the counselee. Moist hands, dry mouth, palpitations of the heart, muscle tension, and insomnia are all evidences of anxiety.

2. Frequent body movements, such as crossing and recrossing the legs, drumming the fingers, rising from the chair, pacing the floor of the counseling room, increasing intensity of movement, or cessation of movement can all be indications of anxiety.

3. The voice reflects a person's emotional state. Tenseness of the voice, shrillness, rapid speech, stuttering, or pauses in speaking are evidences of anxiety.

4. Dress also reflects a person's attitudes, and may be an unconscious means of communication. A well-dressed, well-groomed person usually possesses security and confidence. Striking, inappropriate dress may be evidence of a narcissistic person, often with dependent demands and wishes. Flashy dress or exaggerated makeup often indicates a poor self-image. Slovenly dress--especially if it is a change from the usual--may mean depression. Poor or cheap clothing may not mean poor economic standing, and attractive clothing may or may not mean economic security. One of the paradoxes of America's poor is that they are often well-dressed, but have all the problems of poverty.

5. Slowness of action, or slowness of speech, if they are different from the person's normal responses, may indicate depression.

6. Seductive behavior, in dress, actions, manner of sitting, conversation, or looks, usually indicates insecurity, or sexual maladjustment, sometimes frigidity in women. In men it signifies insecurity, maybe homosexuality. It usually is an evidence of strong transference feelings that should be considered.

7. Where a person sits in a counseling room indicates his relationship to the counselor and the counseling situation. If he takes a chair some distance from the desk, it indicates hesitation and resistance. If he moves the chair closer, or seeks to move closer, it may indicate either fear of rejection or desire for closeness. The desk may frequently be used as a barrier by the counselee. The way the person sits is also significant. Sitting on the edge of the chair, rigid and upright, indicates tension and anxiety.

8. Laughter is a good indication of a person's state of mind. Nervous laughter or giggling indicates tension. Inappropriate laughter, that is, laughter at the wrong things, indicates maladjustment. Free and easy laughter, especially at oneself, is a sign of good adjustment.

9. When a person is consistently late or habitually breaks appointments, it may mean resistance (it may not; maybe he simply could not find a place to park). When a person is early, it sometimes indicates anxiety.

RELATING THEORY TO PRACTICE: Check out the above items in experience. Do a person's body movements, dress, etc. indicate tension as indicated by other facts available about a person?

Add any additional nonverbal clues you may observe or notice.

7. MENTAL AND PSYCHOLOGICAL TESTS

Psychological tests are a common tool of the clinical psychologist, the school counselor, the vocational counselor, and, to some extent, the marriage counselor and psychiatrist. The pastor should not attempt to administer or to score such tests unless he is particularly trained and qualified to do so. He should be aware of the tests that are available. He should know both their values and limitations and should have some acquaintance with basic principles of test interpretation and the use of results in counseling.

There are literally hundreds of psychological tests. Listed below are the general areas, or types of tests, with a few references to some of the most standard and widely used tests.

1. Mental Ability Tests. These are sometimes called IQ tests (which is

unfortunate, for not all give an IQ), and sometimes called intelligence tests. Perhaps the most accurate designation would be scholastic aptitude tests, for more than anything else, they measure the ability to do academic work.

    a. Individual Tests of Mental Ability. The Stanford-Binet; Wechsler-Bellvue Intelligence Scale for Children (WISC); Wechsler Adult Intelligence Scale (WAIS) are the most common. They are individually administered and time-consuming, but quite accurate. The Binet gives an IQ and mental age. The Wechsler gives verbal IQ, quantitative IQ, and a combined IQ.

    b. Group Tests of Mental Ability are the most common kind of psychological tests. They are used by schools, the army, etc. They can be administered to whole groups at one time. Among the most common are: The Otis Quick-Scoring Test of Mental Ability, the California Test of Mental Maturity, Ohio Psychological Examination, Army General Classification Test, etc.

    c. High Level Tests of Mental Ability are used primarily in the selection of graduate school candidates. The Graduate Record and the Miller Analogies are common.

    d. Performance Tests are used to secure an evaluation of those who have language problems, deprived cultural backgrounds, or other limitations in their experience or education.

    e. Special Tests are designed for use with special cases such as the blind, deaf, etc.

2. Educational Skills and Academic Achievement Tests

    a. Educational Achievement Tests measure a student's achievement in certain areas against national norms. Tests and test batteries are available in such subjects as English, Math, Social Sciences, etc., at all levels from the early grades to college. They measure how well a person has used his ability and educational opportunities. They are useful in educational and vocational guidance, college placement, etc.

    b. Reading Tests measure reading rate, comprehension, and vocabulary. They are very useful in academic guidance.

    c. Study Habit Inventories give an indication of a student's study habits and techniques, and locate both strengths and weaknesses. The Wrenn Study Habit Inventory and the Brown-Holtzman are prepared for the college level. The Kemp-Hunt Check List of Study Skills and Attitudes is designed to assist theological students in studying more effectively.

3. Vocational Interest Tests measure one's interest in certain areas. The Kuder Preference Record and others measure interest by general areas, such as scientific, aesthetic, social service, clerical, etc. Others, such as the Strong Vocational Interest Inventory, measure interests in specific vocational areas such as Y.M.C.A. secretary, public accountant, psychologist, etc. The theory is that a person will do better, persist longer, and find greater satisfaction if his vocational choice is in an area in which he is genuinely interested.

4. Vocational Aptitude Tests measure one's potential in certain vocational areas. They predict what one might achieve if he had training. They are used by school counselors, vocational counselors, employment services, etc. Some professions have developed their own tests.

5. Tests of Family Life are used by some marriage counselors in predicting success in marriage and in locating problems in marriage. They consist of temperament surveys such as the Taylor-Johnson Temperament Survey, or the Burgess-Cattrell-Wollin Schedule on Marriage Adjustment which attempt to determine the compatibility of a couple, and the sex-knowledge inventories which measure a person's factual knowledge about sex.

6. Personality Tests are of many kinds and have great divergences of value. They are the most difficult to construct and interpret and should only be used by a skilled clinician.

    a. Self-rating scales, problem checklists, etc. are used by schools and colleges.

    b. Paper and pencil personality tests are used in schools by clinical psychologists, etc. Some such as the Minnesota Multiphasic Personality Inventory, are carefully standardized and give good clues to a person's emotional adjustment. Incomplete Sentence Tests, such as the Rotter, do have a score which indicates neuroticism, but are also useful in giving indications of where problems might occur. (See Memo on the Use of The Incomplete Sentence Blank.)

    c. The projective techniques should only be used by a skilled clinician. The Rorschach Inkblot Test and the Thematic Apperception Test (TAT) are the most common. The subject gives the response to what he sees in a series of inkblots or tells a story of his own creation about a series of ambiguous pictures. These reveal his personality pattern.

Use of Tests

Psychological tests can be very useful as a check on individual evaluation. They can provide information quickly that otherwise might take many interviews to attain. In such areas as mental ability testing they provide information in standardized form so one can make reasonable predictions as to the counselee's academic potential, etc.

Certain principles should guide the use of all tests:

1. Tests should only be administered and interpreted by those qualified and trained to do so.

2. It is usually better for someone other than the counselor to do the testing. Testing is judgmental; counseling is permissive and accepting.

3. Tests should be selected carefully and used only for the purposes for which they were intended.

4. All test information should be evaluated with other means of evaluation, primarily the interview, etc.

5. When there is doubt about test findings, one should retest. Tests can be wrong due to faulty instructions, lack of motivation, etc.

6. No ultimate decision, such as a career choice, or anything else that affects a person's future, should be made on the basis of one test alone.

7. There are some aspects of personality that no tests are designed to measure.

8. Information about test results should be given in the form of general interpretation--rarely in terms of exact scores--and only to the degree the person can understand and accept.

9. It is probably neither wise nor necessary for a pastor to do psychological testing. It confuses the roles in the parishioner's (counselee's) mind, and there are usually other persons available who are trained and qualified to provide such a service.

FOR FURTHER STUDY: There are many things a person can do to understand better such instruments as psychological tests.

1. The best single procedure is to take course work, preferably at the graduate level, in mental tests and measurements. It is only through such procedures that one can be considered qualified for the administration and interpretation of psychological tests.

2. There are many books on testing that can be read. One should choose standard texts such as Cronbach's Essentials of Psychological Testing, or Goldman's Using Tests in Counseling.

3. A pastor can go to a university testing center or to a psychologist and secure copies of the standard intelligence, interest, and personality tests. He can then study their contents and the manuals about them. Note: this does not qualify a person to attempt to administer tests.

RELATING THEORY TO PRACTICE: When a pastor refers a parishioner for tests, or when he goes to a school guidance office to secure test results on a student, he can ask for an interpretation from the psychologist or guidance worker. This should always be done with the counselee's consent, and if a pastor does this regularly he will accumulate considerable understanding of tests and their use.

FOR PERSONAL GROWTH: Arrange to take a battery of psychological tests from a qualified psychometrist or psychologist. This will acquaint you with the contents of tests, it will help you understand how others feel who are taking tests, and the interpretation should help you understand yourself better.

COMMUNITY RESOURCES. List the testing services that are available.

	Name	Phone	Address
School Counseling Service	_____	_____	_____
	_____	_____	_____
University Testing Service (local or nearest community)	_____	_____	_____
Psychologists in private practice	_____	_____	_____

8. EVALUATING INTELLIGENCE

There are occasions when it is important for a pastor to understand the level of a person's intelligence. This is especially true in educational and vocational guidance. Scholastic aptitude and vocational possibilities are determined to a large extent by mental ability. In family counseling a comparative evaluation of the intelligence of two people may be of importance. How can one determine what a person's mental ability is?

1. The best single measure is a standardized mental ability test administered by one qualified to do so.

A student in the public schools usually has been administered a mental ability test. When there is a good guidance department, the tests are administered regularly, giving an opportunity for comparative records. A student in a university is usually given a battery of tests on admission to the university.

Information about a student's test results is usually made available to a pastor if the young person grants his permission. Most school counselors prefer to give an interpretation rather than exact scores, which is as it should be.

Persons not in school can be referred to the testing center of the nearest university or to a clinical psychologist for such tests at a modest fee.

It should be remembered that--

An individual test is more accurate than a group test.

A performance test should be used for those with a language disability or limitation.

Two tests are always better than one. Do not make far-reaching decisions on the basis of one test.

A percentile rank has meaning only when used with specific norms.

It is better to provide an interpretation than an exact score to a counselee.

A high score is more likely to be a true measure than a low score. There are many ways a person may score below his ability; there are very few in which he can score above it.

A low score should always be checked against another test.

A test is always a measure of ability and opportunity. Tests of those with limited cultural backgrounds tell what a person can do, not what he might do with more opportunity.

Standardized tests assume a common background for the group. A foreign student may not get an accurate measure on an American test, for example.

2. Transcripts, grade point averages, or grades themselves give a fairly reliable clue to intelligence. An overall GPA is a better index than a grade in a single course, and a transcript over several years is a better indication than a GPA for one year.

For overachievers or underachievers a GPA may be deceiving and should be checked by standardized tests.

When test scores and the GPA are not similar, one should check carefully for other problems.

A high school transcript is still one of the best predictions of success or failure in college.

3. With adults the educational level that they have completed gives some indication of intelligence. The fact that one did not go to college does not necessarily mean that he did not have college ability. If one completed college, it does mean that he did.

4. One's vocational position and his success in it give a fairly accurate clue to his ability. It should be recognized, however, that adaptational ability, personality factors, etc. also contribute to vocational success. High levels of performance in positions requiring academic effectiveness would not need further testing.

5. Vocabulary is a good clue to ability. People think with words. By listening to a person's conversation one can get an indication of his intellectual ability.

6. The ability to do abstract reasoning is a definite mark of mental ability; the retarded, for example, cannot do this.

7. One's reading, hobbies, and interests give a clue to mental capacity. Again, some people of high intelligence read little, but most of them read rather widely.

It should be pointed out that intelligence alone does not provide self-fulfillment--or even vocational success. Other factors, such as good interpersonal relations, self-acceptance, etc., are equally if not more influential.

FOR FURTHER STUDY: There are a variety of sources that will give a discussion of the nature of intelligence. Any basic introduction to psychology will include a section on intelligence, as will any standard book on educational psychology. Check also the books on mental testing referred to in section 7. Note the material on measuring intelligence.

COMMUNITY RESOURCES: List Testing Services that are available:

	Name	Phone	Address
School Counseling Service	_____	_____	_____
	_____	_____	_____
University Testing Service (Local or nearest community)	_____	_____	_____
Psychologists in private practice	_____	_____	_____

9. EVALUATION AND DIAGNOSIS

Opinions on evaluation vary from those who say that diagnosis is the central fact of counseling to those who say that one should concentrate on the methods he uses, even to the point of evading making a diagnosis. Without entering into this controversy we maintain that both points of view are important. A thorough and accurate evaluation of a counselee and his problems must be made in order to determine what procedures will be followed.

1. Any diagnosis of a person's problems should include his "presenting problem." He is the first and basically the primary source of information. One should always keep in mind the fact that what a counselee states originally may or may not be the real problem. It may not even be the one he wants to discuss. He is testing the counselor, either consciously or unconsciously, as to what he wants to reveal. He may not even know what the problem is. One should be aware not only of what the counselee says, but also of what he does not say.

2. Keep all diagnostic conclusions tentative, especially in the early stages. Since the experts frequently disagree, we cannot be dogmatic. One's evaluation of a situation changes from interview to interview or even within an interview, as new information makes one aware of new aspects of a problem or even of a new problem. Such new information usually comes only when the counselee feels free to express it.

3. Do not attempt to make a definitive medical or psychiatric diagnosis.

Though the situation may appear clear-cut, only a physician can diagnose the symptoms and severity of a physical or mental disease. When evidence of either type of illness is present, insist on a medical examination and diagnosis. Physical symptoms may mask emotional problems and vice versa. A complete medical evaluation is essential in most cases.

4. Utilize all available information in evaluating a counselee: information from the initial interview; information from his church record, personal file, or other sources that will give you such things as his age, educational level, church affiliation, family, etc.; any available test scores; his presenting problem, his evaluation of the situation; any nonverbal clues such as his appearance; the duration and intensity of the problem, etc. Where such information is lacking, secure it if at all possible.

5. Do not force your counselees into preconceived ideas of your own. Some counselors tend to assume that all counselees have sex problems, or feel inadequate, etc. Be objective; check your own biases.

6. When you are in doubt and the situation is serious, check your judgment with a physician, psychiatrist, psychologist, or with another pastor trained in pastoral care. Permission should be received from the counselee for a consultation.

7. Remember that helping people is a continuous process and coincides with the process of evaluation. Help must not necessarily be deferred until an accurate and complete evaluation is made. Alcoholics Anonymous has demonstrated that people can be helped by following a set of definite procedures. The pastoral counselor can help persons by support, reassurance, and guidance, whether or not he understands at the time all of the implications.

8. Evaluation should always be related to counseling procedures; that is its purpose. It is through evaluation that one determines whether a counselee's needs are support, reassurance, interpretation, instruction, or referral. Both evaluation and counseling plans are tentative and subject to constant change.

9. Remember that there is rarely any single cause for a problem. The causes are multiple, complex, interrelated, and often subtle and obscure. Careful listening can usually provide sufficient data for determining the causes.

10. Include in your evaluation your own reaction to the person. Does he arouse interest, hostility, affection, feelings of like or dislike, sexual attraction, protective feelings, etc. This may tell you some things about the counselee. It may help determine whether or not you should be the one to do the counseling.

RELATING THEORY TO PRACTICE: After each counseling interview write out your own diagnosis at that point. Continue through subsequent interviews. Keep a running account of how your evaluation may change as the situation unfolds.

When possible have this checked with a psychiatrist, psychologist, or pastoral counselor.

42

10. ASSESSMENT OF PERSONALITY

In order to help a person it is necessary to be able to make as thorough and accurate an evaluation of his needs and problems as is possible. Only with an adequate evaluation can one determine what procedures one will follow, whether or not one ought to refer, etc. This is a continuing process and is never complete. The following methods of evaluation all have value.

1. Observation. The pastor in the parish has the opportunity of observing the parishioner in social settings, at home, at his place of business, in positions of responsibility. The pastor can be aware of the parishioner's patterns of responding to other people, and of his mood and temperament. Such observations in no wise imply that observing such activity is an attempt to diagnose or evaluate. At a pastoral counseling center there is no such opportunity until the person presents himself. However, even here his manner, the nonverbal clues (see Sect. 6, "Nonverbal Clues") give one an initial evaluation of the person's needs.

2. Evaluation of Others. Employers, teachers, doctors, pastors, friends can make helpful suggestions about a person's needs. However, it must be recognized that their information can also confuse. Their opinions may differ widely and not agree with yours. When a person has had previous counseling or psychotherapy, it is well, with his permission, to secure the other counselor's evaluation of the person, find out why the counseling was terminated, etc.

3. The Presenting Statement. The first description of the person's needs usually comes from the person himself. Whereas the initial statement of need is not the one that may require the most attention, nevertheless, it is the person himself who is seeking help, and his stated concerns are our primary source of information.

4. Case History. A case history includes one's family background, health record, academic and work record, etc. Many case history outlines have been developed. Examples of such blanks may be found in Appendix 3. Such information is almost routinely secured at a counseling center during the intake interview. A pastor may already be familiar with such information about most of his parishioners. When he is not, he can secure it informally through conversation.

5. Consultation. When a pastor is not sure of his own evaluation of a person's needs, he should consult with a specialist. This might be a doctor, psychologist, psychiatrist, or another pastor. The person's permission should be secured for such consultation. The consultation may determine whether the pastor continues with the person as a counselee. In some cases it indicates that the pastor is the one most qualified to do so; in others it may mean referral.

6. Psychological Tests. Psychological tests give a standardized measure of abilities, interests, aptitude, achievement, and emotional adjustment. They are usually fairly complete for a college student. For the high school and elementary student, they vary with the school. An adult will probably have to be sent to a psychologist or a university testing service to be tested. (See Sect. 7, "Mental and Psychological Tests.")

7. Transcripts. A person's academic record gives many clues to his inter-

ests, abilities, motivations, etc. Patterns of grades are more important than individual grades. Changes in level of grades are usually indicative of emotional problems, perhaps of new motivation, etc. Recent grades are usually more significant than earlier grades.

8. Dream Interpretation. The psychoanalysts make much use of dream analysis and interpretation. Freud called dreams "the royal road to the unconscious." It was his book on dreams that gave him worldwide attention. Freud spoke of dreams as wish fulfillments. Jung, Adler, Fromm, and others present different theories. Two analysts studying the same dream may give different interpretations. When the experts disagree, the pastoral counselor must move with caution. He is not trained to do depth therapy or dream analysis. At times a counselee's dreams are clear-cut; there can be little doubt as to their meaning. When a counselee presents a dream and wishes to discuss it, the pastoral counselor explores this behavior as he does any other--in collaboration with the counselee.

9. Slips of the tongue. The familiar "Freudian slip" should always be noted for it can have significance. Again it should be treated with caution. Any interpretation must be seen in the light of the total information one has of the counselee.

10. Autobiography. Many counselors have found it helpful to have the counselee write an autobiography. This is quite different from the case history. In the case history the counselor gathers specific data. In the writing of an autobiography the counselee is requested to write his own story in his own way. It is easier for some persons to write their experiences than to tell them. An autobiography must be evaluated as a conversation is, since some persons may distort the facts, etc. One of the values of the autobiography is that it can reveal feelings not expressed in the case history.

The total evaluation consists of combining elements of all these factors.

FOR PERSONAL GROWTH: Keep a log of observations of behavior for a period of several weeks. Observation can be made anywhere--on the street, at a meeting, or on a call as well as during counseling. Write out these observations, noting facial expressions, tone of voice, and all manifestations of behavior.

RELATING THEORY TO PRACTICE: Develop the practice of securing all the data available about your counselees. Secure as many of the items listed above as possible. Keep records of your own experiences and go over the material with a psychiatrist, psychologist, or pastor trained in pastoral care.

Ask some of your counselees to write an autobiography. Compare what they say about themselves with what you have observed or noted about them.

COMMUNITY RESOURCES. List the persons who are available for consultation and evaluation:

11. PEOPLE UNDER STRESS

People who are under stress respond differently than people under average or normal conditions. Almost everyone who goes to a pastor or a counseling center for help is under some degree of stress or he would not go. Certain factors about people under stress should be kept in mind.

1. Stress is an individual thing. What creates stress for one person may not for another. Stress must be seen from the counselee's perspective. A situation that might not appear as one of stress for the pastor in his own circumstances may create considerable stress for the person in his circumstances.

2. Severe stress brings out the best and the worst in persons. Some may respond to stress with courage and renewed effort, while others may respond to the same situation by fear or withdrawal.

3. People who are under stress or in pain (one form of stress) become egocentric. The central fact of the problem or the pain focuses the person's attention on himself. An extrovert may become an introvert. He may not be interested in others because of his concern about himself at the moment. Such a self-focus is usually transitory and disappears when the stress is relieved.

4. People under stress endow authority figures or those in the helping professions with magical or superhuman powers. They expect them to produce sudden dramatic changes in or solutions to their problems, or they may endow them with the power to destroy.

5. People under stress listen with strange intensity to words and ideas, especially from authority figures. Statements a counselor may make almost casually may be seized upon and remembered and distorted as providing great hope or great discouragement.

6. People under stress often revert to behavior responses of childhood. They may become dependent, cry, pout, become noncommunicative, etc.

7. People under stress have a great sense of urgency, almost of desperation. Their urgency may not be in accord with the facts; they may have more time to work on the problem than they realize.

8. People under stress tend to be confused in their thinking; they over- or underreact; they have difficulty seeing reality.

9. People under stress have difficulty in concentrating. A student may find it difficult to study; an adult may not be able to keep his mind on his job.

10. People under stress have difficulty in interpersonal relationships. They

feel others do not understand them; they may be intolerant of others; they may attempt to hide their stress and to act natural, which only increases the tension.

11. People under stress have difficulty in their religious beliefs and experiences. They attend worship services but find little value in them. They find it difficult to pray, etc., or they may turn to religion with great hope.

12. Stress can thus be viewed in two perspectives, as promoting growth and therefore desirable (where solutions to the stress are probable and possible), or resulting only in frustration and therefore destructive.

FOR FURTHER STUDY: Any of the books in the bibliography on general psychology will have a section on stress. Books on mental health, abnormal psychology and psychiatry will deal with it extensively.

12. BUILDING ON STRENGTHS

"They who wait for the Lord shall renew their strength" (Isa. 40:31a).

This statement of the ancient prophet is emphasized throughout scripture again and again. The book of Deuteronomy gives the assurance one can look to the future with confidence, for "as your days, so shall your strength be" (Deut. 33:25).

Paul expressed his personal faith when he wrote to the Philippians, "I can do all things in him who strengthens me" (Phil. 4:13). This was no idle boast, no grandiose expression, no evading of reality. It was a statement of faith: if a problem must be faced, Paul could face it; if a need must be met, he could meet it. Religion for Paul was a source of strength.

The book of Ephesians puts it in poetic language--actually in the form of a prayer, "For this reason I bow my knees before the Father . . . that according to the riches of his glory he may grant you to be strengthened with might through his Spirit in the inner man, and that Christ may dwell in your hearts through faith" (Eph. 3:14-17).

In both the Old Testament and the New, faith in God, or commitment to Christ, was a source of strength. Throughout the centuries this has been so. Religion at its best has made men strong.

Psychologists and psychiatrists speak of ego-strength, which should result in the courage to be one's self, patience to endure a difficult situation, confidence not to be overwhelmed by circumstances, and willingness to accept responsibility.

The pastor by virtue of his position builds on strengths. The psychiatrist and the physician concentrate predominantly on weakness, pathology, and disease. To say that the pastor specializes in building on strengths does not mean that he ignores weaknesses or the need to eradicate evil or correct error. Many times, if one can build strength, many of the weaknesses (or problems) can be endured or disappear.

William James, in his famous essay "The Energies of Men," said most people have resources of strength that they are unaware of and that can be drawn upon in time of need. Many people who come for counseling have focused so long on their weaknesses that they are unaware of their strengths.

Strength comes from many sources. Physical strength comes from a combination of activity and quiet. Physical strength is increased by exercise; it is restored by rest.

Spiritual strength is increased by service; it is restored by worship. Giving a person a task to do, helping him feel that he is needed, that someone or some cause is depending on him, can increase his strength. There is an old saying that "nothing makes a man strong like a cry for help."

Anything that deepens one's capacity to worship, to pray, or to trust restores strength. "Be strong, and let your heart take courage; yea, wait for the Lord!" (Psa. 27:14.)

To sustain, to support, to reassure another—if it is done realistically—is to produce strength. The knowledge that someone understands and cares is a source of strength. The very word "comfort" comes from two Latin words, cum and forte meaning "with strength."

Faith increases strength, "the assurance of things hoped for, the conviction of things not seen" (Heb. 11:1). Hope increases strength: when hope is diminished, then strength is reduced; when hope is real, strength is produced. Love increases strength. The realization that one is needed, trusted, and loved is a source of strength. This truth is the essence of the Christian experience: "So faith, hope, love abide, these three" (I Cor. 13:13).

These are things about which a pastor should be concerned. To help another person gain a sense of strength may well be one of the most important things he will ever do.

That which is true of the individual is equally true of the family. An article in the Canadian Journal of Mental Health described a project conducted by three family counseling agencies. They tried an experiment in which they focused primarily on family strengths. They did not eliminate or ignore the necessity of dealing with weaknesses; they recognized the necessity of working through hostilities. They also stressed the value of recognizing and developing strengths. Their definition of family strengths was, "Those factors or forces which contribute to family unity and solidarity and which foster the development of the potentialities which are inherent in the family."

They learned that some strengths are obvious, some unnoticed. What is a strength for one may not be for another. They listed several, such as worship, common values, mutual encouragement and support, recreation and leisure, participation in community affairs, communication, a sense of humor, etc. To these we add common vocational goals and the ability to solve problems. There are many more.

Families themselves were encouraged to join in the search for strengths. Many had been used to thinking only in terms of "problems." They found this search a new experience which was in itself strengthening. As they took inventory of their strengths, they became aware of new resources.

The results reported were quite positive. "Only as the casework focus shifted

47

to a search for strengths--however minimal--on which to build were there beginning evidences of movement."

The pastoral counselor should be a specialist in those things that produce strengths.

RELATING THEORY TO PRACTICE: In order that you will develop the practice of considering strengths, review any recent counseling sessions and study any present or future ones with the following questions in mind.

What strengths are present within this family or this individual?
How can the persons involved be helped to realize the strengths they have?
What latent strengths are present that can be recognized or realized?
What new strengths could be developed?
How can these persons develop and utilize potential strengths?

FOR PERSONAL GROWTH: Write out what you feel your own strengths are. Ignore your weaknesses and limitations for this exercise. Concentrate on your strengths.

13. PASTORAL COUNSELING TECHNIQUES

A variety of counseling techniques are available to the pastoral counselor. Historically, pastoral counseling has consisted of exhortation, reassurance, at times, moralizing; and, usually, the giving of advice. With the development of the psychological sciences and the popularity of psychotherapy, pastors have had to re-evaluate and refine their methods. Every pastor must work in his own way. He should be familiar with the various techniques available, know when they are most appropriate, and recognize the values and limitations of each. The particular technique that is used in any interview depends on the needs of the person being counseled and also on the experience and personality of the counselor. One may use different methods with different persons, or different methods with the same person, depending upon what is indicated at the moment. The following suggestions may be helpful.

1. Listening. Listening is almost always useful in the early stages of an interview. In many cases someone to listen to him is all the counselee needs. (See Sect. 5 on "Listening.")

2. Reflection of Feelings. This method, made popular by Carl Rogers, is useful to the pastoral counselor. It fosters acceptance, gives a feeling of being understood, and leads to insight in the counselee. It should be noted that what is

48

being discussed is a "reflection of feelings," not a "parroting" back of intellectual content. With some persons this may arouse resistance and frustration.

3. Questioning. Questioning is sometimes referred to as probing. What is meant is not an obtrusive, overly aggressive use of questions. At times the pastor needs more information, or the counselee needs to weigh alternatives, etc.; these goals can be pursued by asking questions. Open-ended questions are better than Yes or No questions unless one simply wants factual information. Structured questions are sometimes helpful in enabling the counselee to secure a better evaluation of reality.

4. Interpretation. At times the pastor may want to interpret to a person what he feels the person's situation is, what the causes of his behavior are, etc. Interpretation should be attempted with great caution and usually should be tentative. If the counselor is wrong but the counselee accepts his interpretation as fact, the exercise may be more confusing than helpful.

5. Reassurance and Support. These are great resources for the pastor. Because of his symbolic role, he can use them with power. Some persons, especially those with situational problems, may find these to be all they need. However, reassurance and support also should be used with caution. Too much reassurance received too quickly or too easily deprives the person of the right of grappling with his problem, and may even imply that the pastor does not understand him.

6. Confrontation and Advice. Occasionally a person must be confronted with the reality of a situation he is evading, or with the way his behavior affects others, or with the fact that he is wrong. This is never easy (if the counselor enjoys it, he should check his own motives). On the other hand, confrontation is not necessarily negative. It can be very therapeutic. While it is considered better for a person to come to his own insights, there are also occasions when the pastor must make specific statements.

7. Religious Resources. The pastor has available the resources of the Church, the sacraments, prayer, and Scripture, the healing power of religious concepts such as forgiveness, grace, redemption, and salvation (see Sect. 39, "Religious Resources").

FOR FURTHER STUDY: Read in the field of pastoral counseling the writings of Howard Clinebell, Wayne Oates, or Carroll Wise etc., and in the field of general counseling, the writings of McKinney, Rogers, Thorne, etc. Full titles are listed in the Bibliography.

RELATING THEORY TO PRACTICE: Keep a careful record of your counseling or record the sessions on tape. Go back over the record and list in the margin whether you were listening (L), reflecting feelings (R), asking questions (Q), interpreting (I), supporting (S), confronting (C), or using religious resources (RR).

Note which method seems to be predominant in your sessions. In each case ask whether another method might have worked as well or better.

14. TECHNIQUES USED BY SCHOOLS OF COUNSELING AND PSYCHOTHERAPY

There are methods and techniques not frequently mentioned in pastoral care literature which some schools of counseling and psychotherapy have found useful. Some of these the pastor can use. Some he should be aware of because they give insight into human needs. None of these techniques should be attempted by the pastor unless he has schooled himself in the personality theory behind them, is aware of their limitations and dangers, and is trained in their use.

1. Relaxation Therapy. This is based on the findings of Dr. Jacobsen of the University of Chicago. He developed a system whereby his patients are trained to relax by a program of "Progressive Relaxation." The program is widely used by the behavior therapists and learning theorists. The patient is trained in the feeling of tension and the feeling of relaxation. This training extends over a period of weeks. The patient concentrates--sometimes for several days--on one portion of the body, such as the forearm, hand, or wrist. When the whole body has been trained to relax, he finds that most tensions and anxieties disappear. The theory is that one cannot be relaxed and tense at the same time--one condition is incompatible with the other. Other therapists such as Joseph Wolpe use an abbreviated or shorter method of relaxation-training. The counselee is told to focus on one set of muscles in the body and to relax them. He then moves from one set of muscles to the other progressively in one setting until the entire body is relaxed. The person is then told to practice relaxation daily until it becomes somewhat automatic.

2. Assertive Responses. This is also a method of learning theory, particularly of Salter, who makes it the primary technique in his "conditioned reflex therapy." The premise is that if the client can be persuaded to assert himself where hitherto he has been withdrawn or felt inadequate, his anxiety will be inhibited. The counselor points out the irrationality of the client's fears and gives him assertive tasks to do. This is not a great deal different from what pastors have always done when they urged people to make new efforts, etc. Some modify the method by establishing a hierarchy of tasks and working up through them, beginning with the easier ones and moving on to the more difficult. Each successive achievement increases ego-strength.

3. Role-playing. Some therapists create imaginary situations with a client and let him play the roles of his employer, parent, or wife, as the case may be, in order to understand each better. He may be asked to role-play himself in a situation that has been causing him difficulty, so that when he is actually in the situation there may be less tension due to his role-playing practice. At times the counselor may reverse roles and let the counselee become the counselor while he plays the counselee's role. In working with couples a counselor can suggest that the couple do some role-playing and let him observe, perhaps even evaluate and make suggestions. This is not to be confused with role-playing in a group--this is just the counselor and the counselee. There is no reason why the pastoral counselor cannot use such a procedure, providing he feels natural in doing it and does not arouse too much anxiety at any one time.

4. Paradoxical Intention. This is a method advocated by Viktor Frankl as a means of dealing with unnecessary or neurotic anxiety. He suggests that a person actually try to create the situation that he fears, that he "seek out precisely what he fears, and . . .precisely those situations which usually fill him with anxiety." Such a procedure, he contends, makes one aware of the foolish nature of most of men's anxieties and actually eliminates them. Whereas the case studies he cites describe positive results, one should use such procedure with caution.

5. Systematic Desensitization. This method has been developed by the learning theorists, particularly Joseph Wolpe. It utilizes the theory of progressive relaxation mentioned above. First a case history is taken to determine the problem to be dealt with. A hierarchy of anxieties, problems, and goals is constructed, based on the person's case history. Training in progressive relaxation is given the counselee simultaneously with the development of a hierarchy of anxieties. While the person is completely relaxed, the counselor presents scenes to be visualized from the hierarchy. When tension is present, the counselee signals this fact to the counselor, and they do not attempt to go any further that session. Pairing relaxation with what had produced tension desensitizes the counselee to stress situations. Counselor and counselee work through the hierarchy in successive sessions until desensitization has taken place. The key word in this technique is systematic. It must be done carefully and systematically. It is not a technique for the pastor unless he is well trained in learning theory.

6. Self-Disclosure. O. Hobart Mowrer of the University of Illinois advocates that the counselor share with the counselee the fact that he has had the same or similar problems. In his writing on Integrity Therapy he suggests this be done in almost every case. Such "complete openness," as he terms it, leads to a willingness on the part of the client to share his problem and to create a relationship in which it can be resolved. (In Mowrer's case, continued counseling is done with a group.) Others question this procedure, observing that the experiences are never quite the same, and discussing them tends to shift the focus from the counselee to the counselor. There may be occasions when a pastor could use this procedure, but they should be selected with care.

7. Game Analysis (Transactional Analysis). Eric Berne, in his system of psychotherapy called Transactional Analysis, says that the interactions between persons consists of pastimes, games, and scripts. A pastime is a transaction without ulterior motive. A script is an unconscious master plan which determines the overall direction of a person's life. The idea of the game is most useful in pastoral counseling. A game is an ongoing series of transactions, unconscious in nature, and manipulative in procedure, that result in specific, predictable outcomes. Some of the most common are: "If it weren't for you"; "Look how hard I've tried," etc. It provides an interesting, nontechnical way of evaluating relationships which helps people gain understanding of their own behavior.

8. P-A-C: A basic concept of Transactional Analysis is that three states

exist in all people. These are a Parent (P), an Adult (A), and a Child (C), commonly referred to as P-A-C and diagrammed* as follows:

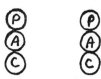

The parent is made up of attitudes received as a child, primarily of a controlling, manipulative nature. The adult is a mature, responsible response pattern. The child is a more dependent, immature response. People respond to other people in one of these three ways.

The transaction that is taking place can be diagrammed by drawing lines connecting the circles. For example, an adult to adult transaction would be as in A-A below. A parental transaction would be as in P-C below. This transaction forces the other person into a child's role. If he wants an A-A transaction the lines cross and problems ensue.

Helping people understand which state they are expressing and how this effects other people   can do much to increase better interpersonal relationships.

9. Hypnosis and Self-Hypnosis. There is a rather widespread interest in the use of hypnosis not only in psychotherapy, but also in obstetrics, minor surgery, and dentistry. Ever since Charcot it has been used in a wide variety of ways in psychotherapy. There is much difference of opinion as to its uses, effectiveness, limitations, and dangers. It has been helpful as a relaxing agent in reducing stress and tension, as a form of suggestion for relieving symptoms in short-term therapy, and as an aid to diagnosis. Some therapists train their patients in self-hypnosis, utilizing tapes and special instructions. Hypnosis is a method of the specialist and is not a tool for the pastor unless he is well trained psychologically. Even then its use tends to confuse his role as a pastor in many people's minds.

Most of the above methods require specialized training and should not be attempted by the pastor unless he has had such training.

FOR FURTHER STUDY: Read the books listed in the Bibliography which discuss the various schools of psychotherapy. For further understanding read the primary sources in each school.

FOR PERSONAL GROWTH: Study the material on relaxation and spend 15 to 30 minutes a day practicing relaxation. It will reduce tension in your own experience and provide an understanding of the values of relaxation therapy.

*The diagrams above are adapted from Figure 2a, p. 30, and Figure 3a, p. 31, in Games People Play: The Psychology of Human Relationships by Eric Berne, M.D. Copyright © 1964 by Eric Berne. Reprinted by permission of Grove Press, Inc., publisher.

COMMUNITY RESOURCES: List any specialists who utilize particular techniques such as hypotherapy, etc.

Name	Phone	Address
_____	_____	_____
_____	_____	_____
_____	_____	_____
_____	_____	_____

15. SUPPORTIVE COUNSELING

Clebsch and Jaekle, in their book Pastoral Care in Historical Perspective, state that when one studies the work of the pastor through the centuries, he finds there have always been four main areas of responsibility for the pastor. These are healing, guiding, sustaining, and reconciling. All are important. We are speaking here of "sustaining."

Sustaining is what is commonly called "supportive counseling," or what some have called in more informal terms the ministry of "standing by." This is a tremendously powerful matter, a service that the minister is uniquely qualified to fulfill, and one that is all some counselees need.

The literature on psychotherapy distinguishes between depth and insight therapy and supportive therapy. Insight therapy usually though not always attempts to explore the past and the present to discover causes for behavior, and to help a person gain insight or understanding of his needs and problems. When properly done it can be very helpful.

There are other occasions when insight therapy is not indicated, when it might even be unkind or dangerous. When the disturbance in a person is very great, or his ego-strength weak, an attempt to gain insight or extend responsibility may not be the best procedure. On such occasions support, reassurance, and strength are the primary need.

What Are Supportive Methods?

Supportive counseling involves many techniques. Just "being there is one. In the parish, pastoral calling often falls in this category. At the church or in a counseling center the technique consists of having the pastor available and having a place where a person can come and discuss his concerns.

Showing genuine concern is another type of supportive counseling. In an impersonal, urbanized society many people have no one who is genuinely concerned about them. The pastoral counselor who can demonstrate sincere concern provides real support to such people.

Listening and reflecting feelings which show one's interest and concern can lend real support.

Asking questions, even taking a personal history, lends some support. This too shows concern.

Validating or confirming to a person the actual or emotional reality of his experience can provide support.

Reassurance, providing it is not superficial and overdone, provides real strength.

Providing information when it is needed, or making suggestions as to possible solutions or procedures can be very supporting.

On occasion, furnishing practical help, especially with the elderly, the young, the foreign-born, or the confused, can have a supportive value beyond the actual help that is offered. The help that is offered may take many forms: shopping for a shut-in, helping someone find a job, etc.

Religious resources, such as prayer, scripture, devotional reading, can be of great help to those for whom they have meaning.

While a pastor's attitudes can hardly be called a technique, his attitudes are perhaps the most influential of all factors. Moods are contagious. If the pastor is nervous, tense, anxious, it will be communicated to the counselee. Quiet, calm assurance can be of great support.

The telephone can be used very effectively in a supportive way. There are persons who cannot get away to come to the office, and many who do not need to be seen every day, or even two or three times a week, but the suggestion that they call and have a brief conversation can be very supportive.

Supportive counseling is often quite informal. On occasion, what the pastor actually does may seem so minimal some would discount it, but it should never be minimized.

Supportive counseling focuses on the present situation, except where a clarification of the past may serve to relieve anxiety or guilt. It does not attempt to probe the past. Its goal is not to produce radical personality change, but to help the person draw on his own inner resources and use them more effectively in meeting his present situation.

Supportive counseling depends greatly on an understanding relationship. (See Section 3, "The Pastoral Counseling Relationship.") A good relationship is a powerful force. It does give one the feeling he is understood; it helps a person gain perspective; it provides reassurance and increases strength.

Like all things supportive counseling can be misused. It can foster dependency feelings, particularly if the counselor uses it to exploit the patient, or to increase his own ego-needs. Too much reassurance can be superficial and can weaken rather than strengthen the counseling relationship.

Elements of support are probably present in every counseling relationship, and in most cases they are valuable. It does not mean they are the only method. When other procedures, such as insight counseling, or referral, are called for, they should be utilized.

When Is Supportive Counseling Indicated?

1. In situational problems, such as crisis situations or periods of temporary stress. In some cases this is only a temporary procedure and may lead to more intensive counseling at a later time.

2. In long-term problems where the person does not need intensive therapy but does need occasional support.

3. With persons where insight would be too threatening. If the actual reality would be so extremely traumatic it would create more tension than it would resolve, then support is indicated.

54

4. With situations that cannot be changed, such as old age, long convalescence, etc.

5. With a person whose husband (or wife, as the case may be), is in intensive therapy, perhaps hospitalized. The husband or wife may not need depth therapy, but he or she does need support.

FOR PERSONAL GROWTH: State in your own words those things that provide courage and strength to a person.

RELATING THEORY TO PRACTICE: Consider each case with these questions in mind: Does this person need support? How can it be provided?

16. INSIGHT COUNSELING

Most of the people who go to a pastor or a counseling center go because they are confused, discouraged, or anxious, or because they feel guilty, inadequate, or angry. Many of these feelings can be relieved. More mature, constructive Christian feelings and actions can be made possible if people can be helped to understand why they feel as they do, what caused their difficulties, and what are the reasons for their feelings and conduct. This is traditionally known as "insight."

"Insight" has many definitions. According to the Encyclopedia of Mental Health the ordinary usage of the term insight refers to "the capacity or act of understanding a situation, other people, or oneself, and the ability to apprehend meaning and relationships of data that are presented."*

1. Generally speaking, the better the insight, the better the prognosis.

2. There are a variety of methods of helping a person to gain insight. The most common are:

      a. Listening, which draws off emotion and enables a person to organize and clarify his feelings.

      b. Interpretation, which gives a person possible explanations for his behavior.

      c. Reflection of feelings, which enables a person to evaluate his own feelings free from threatening or inhibiting situations.

      d. Confronting the person with inconsistencies and contradictions.
(See Section 14 for further definition of some of these techniques.)

3. Some insight may be superficial and may help a person feel better momentarily, but the old problem will return. Some may be deep and profound and lead to significant change. Insight is usually relative and may be difficult to attain. The counselor, therefore, works patiently and persistently.

4. The counselor often has insight into a person's problem ahead of the counselee. It may not be advisable to discuss insight too soon. This can be threatening. Timing is important.

*(Franklin Wells, 1963), III, 850.

5. Insight should not be hurried. People come to insight at their own pace. To force it too fast may create resistance.

6. Generally, it is undesirable to attempt to force insight on another or to try to give insight to another, although under some circumstances it is necessary and useful. The counselor's task is to help the person attain his own insight.

7. Insight may not guarantee improvement. Some people understand their behavior but do not have sufficient motivation to change.

8. Insight is not always indicated as the goal to be sought. There are situations where insight might be too threatening or too painful to be pursued. There are other situations where it is not necessary. Support and reassurance may be all that is required.

9. Some persons can attain insight better than others. Small children are not expected to attain self-understanding as is described here. The elderly often have difficulty attaining insight although this is not always true. Generally speaking, the higher the level of intelligence, the better the possibilities of insight, while the retarded--those in the lower level of intelligence--have difficulty attaining insight. The lower the socioeconomic level of the counselee, the less effective is insight counseling. The reality pressures are so great they tend to respond more to action-oriented methods, although there are always exceptions to all of these.

10. The ultimate goal is not only to help a person attain understanding, but also to put his understanding into action; to replace inappropriate, negative, or positive feelings and behavior with more mature, creative, self-actualizing behavior.

FOR PERSONAL GROWTH: Since insight is so all-important, make out your own definition of insight and list the ways in which insight can be attained.

RELATING THEORY TO PRACTICE: Study your counseling records. Note any indications of insight; list the degree of the person's insight.

17. APPLICATION OF BEHAVIOR MODIFICATION TO PASTORAL COUNSELING

Learning theory has had a strong influence on counseling procedures in recent years. A term often associated with the application of learning theory to therapy is behavior modification, which has developed a school (in fact, schools) of its own. Certain emphases of the learning theorists can be applied to pastoral counseling. Some of their basic tenets or principles are as follows.

1. All behavior is learned behavior. It has been conditioned and reinforced through many repetitions over a long period of time. This would be true of good behavior, as well as maladaptive or neurotic behavior.

2. What has been learned can be unlearned or modified. This is called extinction. New and better modes of responding and behaving can be learned.

3. The goals are to extinguish the neurotic, maladaptive behavior and to develop by reinforcement all healthy or positive behavior.

4. Learning takes place by small steps. One does not attempt to gain his final goals all at once.

5. Each move toward health should be reinforced, rewarded, and strengthened.

6. Regressive, negative, neurotic behavior should be ignored or corrected. One should be careful not to give too much emphasis to negative behavior; in giving too much attention to it one may actually reinforce it.

7. A series of steps or tasks is assigned for one to do. One should start with the simpler ones where success is likely, and reward all positive results.

8. As the counselee experiences success, this will increase his self-confidence and self-esteem and reinforce his willingness to continue the process.

9. Many methods are used to produce results: instruction, modeling the role, assertive techniques, relaxation training, systematic desensitization, etc. (See Sect. 13, Counseling Techniques.)

10. All methods should be carefully planned and pursued systematically.

Some learning theory principles can be applied to other methods of counseling, such as insight or supportive counseling. Some can be used as a supplement to these procedures. For example, one can (a) establish a list of goals or tasks to be attained; (b) arrange them in a hierarchy according to their difficulty, beginning with the easiest and working on through to the more difficult; (c) work out some of these between sessions, some within the counseling periods; and (d) reinforce all growth by praise and encouragement. (Some of these methods are described in Sect. 14.)

FOR FURTHER STUDY: Read any of the books on Behavior Modification or Learning Theory listed in the Bibliography. Pay particular attention to the writings of Wolpe, Ullmer, and Krasner.

RELATING THEORY TO PRACTICE: Study any case records you have available, asking three specific questions: (1) How much of the person's behavior can be called learned? (2) What behavior patterns need to be extinguished? and (3) What expressions of behavior (either verbal or nonverbal) should be reinforced?

COMMUNITY RESOURCES: List persons who use such methods as systematic desensitization, relaxation therapy, and other learning techniques.

Name	Phone	Address

18. THE SEARCH FOR MEANING

Viktor Frankl says that "the search for meaning in life is the taproot of human striving." This is the position of those who belong to the schools known as "existential psychotherapy" or "logotherapy," as Frankl calls his approach. Frankl's approach is an attempt to relate and apply philosophy to man's perplexities by focusing on man's search for the meaning of his existence. The close relationship between such an approach and the historic efforts of the pastor and the theologian are obvious. In fact, we could say that the search for meaning is perhaps the primary emphasis of the pastoral counselor.

Many people who go to a pastor or a counseling center lack meaning and purpose in their lives. Some go because of their very complex problem. The pastor is always concerned about meaning and takes his position from a particular stance, that of the Christian faith. Certain principles that are generally accepted by this school of thought are of importance here.

1. Every man is unique and must find meaning that is real for him in his own situation. Responsibility for this is shared by the counselor as well as the counselee.

2. Emphasis is placed primarily in the present. Little time is spent in probing the past. The basic emphasis is, "What meaning can be found now?"

3. The pastor, like the existential therapist, utilizes any or all methods that contribute to the goal. There are no methods that are unique to existential therapy. Any method that increases the sense of meaning is appropriate.

4. This "search for meaning" emphasis, or this approach can be used either with individuals or with groups. The goals are the same.

5. Some meaning can be found in any situation, even the most difficult or discouraging. This is a statement of faith, but it is all important.

6. Meaning is not found primarily by catharsis or persuasion, but often by confrontation and challenge.

7. The pastor's goal is to discover and release the meaning that already exists by virtue of the fact that the counselee is a child of God.

8. Meaning is ultimately found not through intellectual processes alone, but by action and commitment. It depends not only on understanding, but also on decision and dedication.

FOR FURTHER STUDY: Read the writings of the existential therapists listed in the Bibliography. Pay particular attention to the works of Rollo May and Viktor Frankl.

RELATING THEORY TO PRACTICE: Study your records, asking in each case what meaning has the person found in this experience? What meaning could be found?

COMMUNITY RESOURCES: List any existential therapists in your community.

Name	Phone	Address
_____	_____	_____
_____	_____	_____
_____	_____	_____

19. GUIDANCE AND PASTORAL CARE

Guidance is a public school term. Every good school system employs guidance counselors. The guidance movement has developed its own principles and techniques, training program, and a sizable body of literature. There are occasions when the pastor plays a guidance role.

Guidance is defined by the National Education Association as the "high art" of helping young people "plan their own actions wisely, in the full light of all the facts that can be mustered about themselves and about the world in which they will work and live."*

Johnson, Steffler, and Edelfelt, in a standard text, Pupil Personnel and Guidance Services, state that guidance services are primarily five in number. They list the following:

a. "The individual inventory service is one of gathering, recording, and making available information about a pupil which will be useful to those teaching or counseling him.

b. The information service consists in the provision of up-to-date and accurate information, whether vocational, educational or personal-social.

c. The counseling service provides individual help in making decisions about personal problems.

d. The counseling service aids in putting pupils into appropriate jobs or educational settings.

e. The evaluation service is sometimes referred to as the research service or the follow-up service."**

It is obvious from these definitions that guidance services focus heavily on making decisions, planning educational and vocational careers, using information, weighing alternatives, making choices, developing skills, and carrying plans to

*Gail F. Farwell and Herman J. Peters, Guidance: A Developmental Approach (Rand McNally, 1959), p. 2.
**Walter J. Johnson et al, Pupil Personnel and Guidance Services (McGraw-Hill, 1961), p. 15.

59

their completion. The ideal goal is to assist a person to attain his optimum development. There are times when a pastor is called upon to assist in making decisions, developing plans, etc. He certainly is interested in optimum development.

Guidance can cover many areas. In some areas the pastor is uniquely qualified. These areas include religious guidance, guidance in religious beliefs and practices, guidance for church vocations, premarital guidance, moral and ethical guidance, and some aspects of educational and vocational choice and planning.

Certain guidelines should be observed.

1. To guide, according to the dictionary, means "to indicate, to point out, to show the way." It does not mean making the decision for a person; rather, helping a person understand himself and the alternatives, so that he can make his own decisions.

2. Guidance may include or require insight or supportive counseling. Sometimes a person cannot make a decision or pursue plans until certain emotional problems are worked through.

3. All guidance should be based on as full a knowledge of an individual as is possible. For students, this includes test scores, GPA., the evaluation of teachers, etc. For people not in school, one should secure as much data as is necessary for the decision or problem being discussed.

4. Guidance requires information. Some decisions cannot be made, some plans cannot be completed without adequate information. This does not mean that the pastor must have complete knowledge about all jobs, careers, and educational opportunities. It does mean he must know where such knowledge is available. He must be sure the information is accurate, up-to-date, and complete. Inaccurate or incomplete information may do more harm than good.

5. When it is indicated, one should work in collaboration with school guidance workers, whether at the elementary, secondary, or college level. In most of these cases, the pastor must take the initiative. Many young adults, school dropouts, and older persons have guidance problems but have no guidance worker available other than the pastor.

6. With some persons who come for counseling the guidance approach is the one method that is indicated as being the most effective. Some persons require an authority figure to give guidance and direction. The counselor should always be aware of both the limitations and possible dangers of assuming such a role but not be unprepared to do so.

7. It should be recognized that guidance is a process that takes time. It is most effective when done over a period of time. The making of choices, development of plans, and training in skills can usually only be done over a period of time. One gathers information, explores the possibilities, and allows for the maturation of ideas, then makes decisions or gains the benefits of growth.

8. One should always be aware of the far-reaching importance of guidance functions. While guidance activities may not be as dramatic as some other areas of counseling and psychotherapy, and while there is a tendency to belittle guidance in comparison with other areas of counseling, one should never lose sight of the fact that when one is helping another choose and plan for an educational career, a home, or a vocation, he is dealing with that person's whole future happiness and the contribution he will make to society.

FOR FURTHER STUDY: Read some of the books on guidance listed in the Bibliography. This will help you understand the school counselor and his approach and will include much that can be applied to pastoral counseling.

RELATING THEORY TO PRACTICE: In each case where you are working with a high school, junior high, or junior college student, secure the student's permission to go over his record with the school counselor or guidance worker.

COMMUNITY RESOURCES: List the school counselors and guidance workers in your community.

	Name	Phone	Address
Junior High	_____	_____	_____
	_____	_____	_____
High School	_____	_____	_____
	_____	_____	_____
Junior and Senior Colleges	_____	_____	_____
	_____	_____	_____

20. EDUCATIONAL GUIDANCE AND ACADEMIC PROBLEMS

When a church has a large youth group, or is located in the proximity of a college, it is only to be expected that some will come to the pastor with educational problems. Their academic concerns may be incidental to their problems, they may be interrelated, or, on occasion, they may be the main problem.

Academic achievement depends upon four related factors: (1) ability, (2) motivation, (3) study skills, and (4) reasonable freedom from stress.

Ability is all important. The higher one goes on the educational scale the more ability is demanded. One cannot do academic counseling without a knowledge of the person's abilities or scholastic aptitude. (See Sect. 8, "Evaluating Intelligence.") One would deal with a person who has a low grade point average and low abilities quite differently than if he had a low grade point average and high abilities.

Ability tells what a person can do; motivation determines what he will do. His interests and motivations determine the fields he will enter, whether or not he will persist in the face of discouragement, etc.

Reasonable freedom from stress is necessary for optimum results. Some stress is good; it increases effort, promotes study, etc. Undue stress destroys concentration, inhibits participation in class, etc. Some stress causes a person to prepare carefully for an exam; too much stress may cause a person to "freeze" in an exam.

If a person's abilities are not commensurate with his academic goals, if he lacks motivation, or if he is under such stress he cannot function academically, then general, not academic counseling, is indicated.

Several things should be mentioned concerning this broad subject.

1. Academic counseling involves many things, a knowledge of course requirements, prerequisities, requirements for admission to college or graduate school, study skills, reading rate, scholarships available, etc. One should not give information in such areas unless he is absolutely sure. Misinformation or incomplete information can be misleading. There are persons in the community who can provide the needed information either to the student or the counselor.

2. Much is known about study habits, skills, and techniques. These have been the subject of exhaustive research and experimentation. Such research also has indicated that few college students or graduate students follow the skills that would enable them to function at their optimum level.

3. One of the most common weaknesses in studying is poor use of time. The good students usually schedule and budget their time. They distribute their study throughout the semester and outline requirements well in advance, thus allowing for the maturation of ideas.

4. Having a regular time and place for study, even for specific courses, reinforces concentration and enables a student to get into a topic quicker; spaced study periods are better than long, drawn-out ones. More will be retained from three one-hour periods spaced throughout the week than from one four-hour period at one setting.

5. Reading is such a vital part of academic skills that reading skill should always be checked. Most schools can test reading rate and comprehension. The developmental reading program in schools of education can produce dramatic results in reading skills.

6. Many other factors influence academic achievement. Physical factors should be taken into account, eyesight, hearing, general physical health. Also cocurricular activities, and other outside interests influence academic achievement. How much time and energy is consumed in social activities, church activities, athletics, or employment?

7. Academic interest is highly correlated with one's goals and aspirations. It must be recognized that goals and aspirations may be highly neurotic and unrealistic, and may produce unfortunate results in other areas. Most people are motivated to study when they see some personal or practical gain to come as a result-- most people are not motivated to do so if they do not.

8. Some helpful reading materials for both students and counselors are available in the libraries of most universities.

FOR FURTHER STUDY: Read the sections concerning learning skills in any introduction to educational psychology. Check the nearest school library for materials on study habits.

RELATING THEORY TO PRACTICE: Use the checklist on study habits found in Appendix 5 with each young person who is having academic difficulties. Check with the school counselor for an evaluation of his mental abilities, achievement tests, and GPA.

FOR PERSONAL GROWTH: Study the material on study habits in Appendix 5. Develop a study plan and work out a schedule for your own study. It will increase your effectiveness and help you understand the possibilities for your counselees.

COMMUNITY RESOURCES: List the academic specialists in your community.

	Name	Phone	Address
School counselors Junior High	_____	_____	_____
	_____	_____	_____
Senior High Junior and Senior College	_____	_____	_____
	_____	_____	_____
Developmental Reading Study Habits Test	_____	_____	_____
	_____	_____	_____

Pastoral Aid and Loan Materials:

_____

_____

_____

21. PREMARITAL COUNSELING AND GUIDANCE

More and more couples are turning to pastors for premarital guidance, as well as just asking him to conduct the wedding. Some couples are having problems and want help. Some just want information to prepare them for making a home as best they can. There are three aspects of premarital preparation that should be kept in mind. They are premarital education, premarital guidance, and premarital counseling. All overlap.

Premarital Education. There is a great deal of information available about marriage and the family. Some couples that appear quite sophisticated are limited in the knowledge they possess. This can be provided through conversation, through suggested reading, or in groups. Classes in marriage are available in churches and social agencies. Groups can be organized at the church or a counseling center when they are needed or requested.

The information sought should include such areas as the biblical and historical backgrounds of the family, the place of the family in our changing culture, an understanding of masculine and feminine roles, the relationship of vocational choice and adjustment to family life, the meaning and values of money and the principles of family finance, an understanding of one's sexuality and a Christian interpretation of sex, the sacredness of parenthood, the relationship with in-laws, the capacity to resolve problems, the relationship of the church and the home, and of religious and family life.

Premarital Guidance. Guidance could be called individualized instruction. Here an individual or a couple takes the principles outlined in the preceding paragraphs and develops a plan or program of their own. For example, they may learn the principles of family finance. Through guidance they develop a budget that fits their needs and is within their resources. The same thing is true of relationships with in-laws, the church, etc. These may be emotionally stressful for some and not for others. They always must be oriented to a couple's particular needs and resources.

Premarital Counseling. Counseling is indicated when anxiety, doubt, guilt, hostility, or other negative emotions are causing tension or uncertainty. Education is indicated when information is needed. Guidance is indicated when specific plans and procedures need to be worked through. Counseling is indicated when problems arise, when undue stress is present, when unusual or unique concern must be worked through.

Principles and Procedures

1. The wedding service itself can be a useful tool in helping couples face the seriousness and sacred nature of marriage. A study and discussion of the ideas expressed can be very fruitful.

2. Both separate and joint sessions are indicated for most couples. It is well to have individual sessions so the person is free to express any personal concerns that he or she would be hesitant to state otherwise. Joint sessions are necessary to observe the interaction between the two.

3. When unusual, complicated, or difficult problems are present, such as great differences in age, opposition of the family, or extreme differences in cultural backgrounds, it is well to advocate more counseling time in order that these feelings can be worked through.

4. In interfaith marriages in which the religious differences are great and the religious feelings are strong, each person must work through his own religious commitment. A full and frank discussion is required so that all implications are understood. The universals, or common elements, should be discussed as well as the differences. Do not let the couple take the position that religion does not matter. It does. Their task is to work out a solution that takes into account, but transcends their differences.

5. The pastor should insist upon a medical examination for each person, other than the minimum of a blood test.

6. Some aspects of sex may be dealt with more adequately by the doctor in connection with the medical examination. Frequently doctors only discuss the biological aspects of sex and do not provide an emotional and spiritual interpretation of sex. There is some published material available which can be read and discussed by the pastor and the couple.

7. Some psychological tests and inventories can be useful and clarify situations. The Taylor-Johnson Temperament Analysis and the Sex Knowledge Inventory are available and are the two that are rather widely used.

8. When people do not have adequate time for marriage counseling before the ceremony, it can be done with equal effectiveness after marriage. In fact, in the first few weeks immediately following the marriage a couple may be very receptive to such counseling.

FOR FURTHER STUDY: Read in the general field of family life and in the specific area of premarital counseling and guidance.

RELATING THEORY TO PRACTICE: Have couples take the Taylor-Johnson Temperament Analysis. Go over the material first with a marriage counselor, then with the couple.

COMMUNITY RESOURCES: List the persons in the community qualified to administer the Taylor-Johnson and other such tests, as well as serve as a source of referral for difficult cases.

	Name	Phone	Address
Family Service Agency	_____	_____	_____
Marriage Counselor	_____	_____	_____
Doctor	_____	_____	_____

Pastoral Aid Materials for loan as supplements to counseling:

_____

_____

_____

22. FAMILY COUNSELING

Several research projects have been conducted on the problems people take to their pastor. Almost without exception they indicate that family problems are the most frequent.

Family problems are primarily problems of relationship and can be extremely complex. Any one or all of the following matters should be kept in mind.

1. Is it a family problem, or is the family difficulty a result of one or more emotional illnesses that need treatment? If extreme emotional problems are present, psychiatric treatment may be indicated before family counseling can be expected to be helpful.

2. Are physiological problems present? Women in the middle-age bracket may have emotional accompaniments of menopause that greatly affect family life. A medical consultation is always indicated. While men do not have a physiological menopause like women, they very often have an emotional one.

3. Is the problem a situational one, where a family primarily needs support through a difficult situation, or does it indicate the need for insight counseling?

4. Is the problem due to inaccurate or inadequate information? Many people, even in our sophisticated generation, do not have accurate knowledge about sex, parenthood, family financing, etc. There is a great deal of information about family life available. Some can be given verbally, some by reading. Very rarely is lack of information the sole cause of the problem.

5. Is the problem due to outside, or external, influences, such as interference of in-laws, employer, etc.? On occasion the persons compounding the problems may be contacted; usually they are not available, and one must do the best one can with the ones that can and will receive help.

6. What is the sexual knowledge, history, adjustment? Are there evidences of maladjustment? Perversion? Is there evidence of impotence, frigidity? These conditions must be approached with discretion in pastoral counseling. Their presence may indicate referral to a doctor, they may not. Sex is so much a symptom of a relationship that many times sexual problems improve as other problems are worked through.

7. What is the financial situation in the family? Is the family under financial strain? Are there agreements as to the making, use, and spending of money? Is money being used as a weapon? Money is a clue to one's values, and the use a family makes of money can tell the pastor much about their philosophy of life.

8. Is there agreement about vocational goals? Are both husband and wife employed? Is there agreement about the wife's working? If there are two incomes, is there agreement about how finances are divided or used?

9. What were the motivations for the marriage? Genuine love? Desire to get away from home? Pregnancy? Infatuation?

10. What has been the emotional history of the marriage? Satisfaction? Conflict? Tension? Jealousy? Domination? Reward? What was characteristic of the early years? Have there been good periods? Are there good periods now?

11. Is there agreement about children? The number? Discipline of? Control of? Is there jealousy over children? Concern? Anxiety?

12. What is the degree of emotional maturity? Marriage counselors list immaturity as one of the primary problems. Are there evidences of other emotional factors that may influence the marriage: jealousy, fear of failure, or feelings of inadequacy?

13. Are there agreements or conflicts about role relationships and responsibilities? In Eric Berne's terms, are they playing the role of parents? Adults? Children?

14. What is the degree of communication? Have lines of communication been kept open, broken, destroyed, or exploited?

15. What were and are their expectations in marriage? What do they expect of each other? What was the model in their own homes?

16. Are there common recreational interests, enjoyments, hobbies; things they enjoy together?

17. Are there major differences in backgrounds--cultural, economic, educational, religious? Do these differences cause conflict? Inferiority? Tension?

18. Are there unusual differences in age or physical attractiveness?

19. Has the history of the marriage been good? Difficult from the beginning? Characterized by much conflict? Intermingled by separation or infidelity? Have there been periods free of conflict? Periods of great satisfaction?

20. What strengths are evident? Latent? Could be developed?

21. Are there common ideals and moral values? Extreme differences? If there are differences, is there tolerance of the other's view?

22. What is the religious atmosphere of the home? Is religion a uniting or dividing influence? Are family members active in church? Is religion merely a form, or is it a vitalizing part of life?

Guidelines or Rules of Thumb

Very seldom is the first statement of the problem the central or main one. The counselor should continuously be making assessments.

Family counseling takes time. The people involved should be informed of this. The counselor must anticipate this. The problems have been years in development; they usually are not resolved in a hurry.

The pastor does not assume the position of judge. His purpose is to create understanding, restore healthy communication, build on strengths, foster forgiveness and love.

Ultimate decisions remain with the persons themselves. The pastor attempts to help people understand, weigh alternatives, and correct faulty thinking, but final decisions must be the person's own decision.

There are many patterns of family counseling, each one claiming, and no doubt experiencing, success. The traditional method is to see the individuals separately at first. This enables them to verbalize all their grievances, lowers much anxiety and hostility, and helps them understand their own role and accept their own responsibilities. It usually leads to joint sessions where the counselor can see the interaction and can interpret and assist in developing a deeper level of adjustment. Some prefer to start with the couple together and then they may or may not see them individually. The approach known as conjoint family therapy brings together the entire family constellation, including children and in-laws when they are involved. It should be pointed out this involves some real risk and should only be done when the pastor has had supervised training in such procedures.

FOR FURTHER STUDY: Read material in (a) Family Life, (b) Marriage Counseling.

RELATING THEORY TO PRACTICE: Follow the same procedures suggested in Premarital Counseling.

COMMUNITY RESOURCES:

	Name	Phone	Address
Family Service Agency			
Marriage Counselor			
Doctor			

Pastoral Aid Materials:

_____

_____

_____

23. FILIAL THERAPY

Many persons who go to a pastor or a counseling center go because they are having problems with their children, or are concerned about their children. A pastor is not a child specialist, unless he has had special training. There are agencies in most communities where such services are available.

When a child is seriously disturbed, he should always be referred to a child specialist. One of the most helpful services we can render to parents is to make them aware of these services and help them to accept them.

There are other occasions when a referral may not be indicated, or when it is necessary to help parents while they are waiting to be admitted into a regular proram.

Filial Therapy is the process by which parents are helped to deal with their children. The counselor may or may not see the child at all. The parents are given certain methods and principles to follow.

1. Parents should be helped to understand that all behavior is caused. Even misbehavior is a cry for understanding and help. Misbehavior is often caused by feelings of loneliness, boredom, inadequacy, guilt, etc.

2. Parents should be informed of the usefulness of listening to their children. Many do not listen. Just to establish this pattern can be helpful.

3. Parents should be helped to empathize with their children. They should be taught to sense the importance of feelings and to attempt to understand feelings.

4. Parents should be helped to keep all channels of communication open.

5. Parents should be helped to set some reasonable limits and goals for their children. Children need freedom but within structure. They should not have goals imposed upon them that are unrealistic or unattainable.

6. Parents should be taught the importance of rewarding every achievement, each step toward achievement, all good behavior, and every move toward responsibility and health.

7. Parents should be helped to develop patterns of discipline that do not produce hostility, that do not reward misbehavior. Parents should be warned against the dangers of sarcasm, discipline that is punitive or is more a result of the parent's anger than of his desire to correct or help. There may be occasions when it is necessary to restrain a child from misbehavior when no punishment would be indicated. There may be times when it is best to ignore some behavior rather than let it become a means of getting attention, etc.

8. Parents should be helped to see the importance of being consistent in all the above items. Consistency in both reward and discipline is extremely important.

9. Parents should be given the opportunity to express their feelings and concerns. This may be done in a counseling session, on occasion, in a group, or even by telephone, enabling them to be more relaxed and consistent with their children.

FOR FURTHER STUDY: Study behavior modification techniques as they are described in books on learning theory. Pay particular attention to chapters describing experiments and research with children.

PASTORAL AID MATERIALS: List any books on parent-child relationships. Include Public Affairs Pamphlets or Science Research Associates pamphlets. People are more likely to read a pamphlet than a book.

_____
_____
_____
_____

24. COUNSELING WITH ADOLESCENTS

The majority of people who seek pastoral counseling are adults, but some adolescents seek counseling. Some go to a pastor at the request of their parents. Counseling adolescents is no different methodologically from counseling adults. (See Section 14 on Techniques.) Certain guidelines or principles should be kept in mind:

1. The pastor should not attempt to duplicate or take the place of a child guid-

ance clinic or the school guidance services. When the nature of the problem indicates that these or other services are needed, the pastor should help the adolescent understand and accept the use of them.

2. It is usually better if parents know an adolescent is receiving counseling. There may be exceptions when a young person is seen temporarily without the parent's knowledge, but they would be rare.

3. One of the most helpful services that can be rendered to adolescents is to help their parents understand their needs and problems and to develop patterns of communication and relationships that will reduce tension and increase understanding. (See Section 23, Filial Therapy.)

4. The pastor should not attempt to talk the current language of the teen-ager. He should not talk down to the teen-ager. He should not try to impress him with technical terms. He should be natural. He may find this difficult to do. Adults project into adolescents their own conflicts, their own hopes and fears. We as counselors must clarify our own feelings to ourselves so we may meet the adolescent at his point of difficulty.

5. The pastor should remember that our culture is very difficult for an adolescent. The so-called generation gap is almost ubiquitous. Conflict between parents and siblings is not unusual, or necessarily serious. Both parents and teen-agers need guidance and support. Growth through adolescence leads to separation from parents and siblings. This is usually painful for parents as well as for adolescents. It is necessary for maturity to take place, but the adolescent approaches separation with ambivalent feelings.

6. Adolescence is a time of decision-making. Young people are making choices that will affect their entire future; the choice of a life partner; the choice of an educational program; the choice of a career or vocation; the choice of a life philosophy. Some make these choices quite easily, some with great difficulty.

7. The pastor should remember that the adolescent probably sees him as a representative of the adult world. It is a cultural pattern to be resistant to those over thirty years of age. In some cases the adolescent's treatment by adults has been unfortunate. He automatically responds with initial resistance.

8. Adolescence is a time of tremendous transition--from childhood to maturity; from prepubertal bodily functions to adult bodily functions; from school to work; from dependence to independence; from the parental home to marriage, etc. Through it all the adolescent is coming to a concept of self, to a sense of his own identity, personally, socially, sexually, vocationally, spiritually.

9. The pastor should not see adolescents as stereotypes. Each has his own individuality. Individual differences must be observed. Each has different abilities, interests, aptitudes, backgrounds, rates of maturity, ideals, values, ambitions, personality traits, etc.

10. All adolescents have basic needs that must be met (as do all other age groups, for that matter). These are such things as attention, affection, acceptance, a sense of achievement. One of the functions of the counselor is to help the young person meet these needs.

11. Adolescence is characterized as a time for religious doubt. Young people

challenge the church, the clergy, the religion of their parents. Sometimes a revolt against the church is one way they can show resistance to their parents. Sometimes it is done to help the relationship with their peers. Others are wistfully seeking for something to believe. Religion cannot be imposed upon them. They can be helped to work through their own questions and come to a point of commitment. Emotionally they want to belong and to become committed to something important. Religious experience that is meaningful is more "natural" for a young teen-ager than "unnatural."

12. Adolescence is important because a person's whole future is involved. Resolving an immediate problem is necessary; planning for the future may be more far-reaching.

FOR FURTHER STUDY: Read some of the basic texts on the Psychology of Adolescents.

COMMUNITY RESOURCES: List specialists with children and youth.

	Name	Phone	Address
School Counselors			
Child Guidance Clinic			
Child psychiatrists			

25. PRINCIPLES OF REFERRAL

A basic premise of all pastoral counseling is that everyone with whom the pastor counsels will receive the best service that is available. This includes helping him find other sources of help when a need for them is indicated. The following guidelines should be observed.

1. The welfare of the individual or family is the primary consideration. The pastor should never attempt to do what someone else can do better.

2. If the person needs training or resources (funds, equipment, facilities) that the pastor does not have, the pastor should refer him to the proper person or agency. If the pastor does not have the time to deal with the problem adequately, he should refer. If the pastor's relationship with the person is so close or so strained it would impair effective counseling, he should refer.

3. A person should be prepared in advance for the possibility of a referral, maybe in the first interview. Whenever it seems that a referral is needed soon, one should begin to prepare the counselee for it.

4. Many times the pastor's role is to help the person accept the idea of referral, eliminate feelings of guilt, embarrassment, unworthiness that accompany going to an agency or to a specialist. Many people have "emotional blocks" against referral that need to be removed before an actual referral to specific agencies, individuals, or professions can be made.

5. Recognize that there is a "readiness" for referral. At times persons need to accept the referral "emotionally." At times more information about an agency is necessary. On occasion, the counselor must continue until the person can accept the referral--unless there are major contraindications.

6. A person has the right to know the reason for the referral.

7. A person has the right to be informed about the nature and function of an agency, its fees, waiting period, etc. He should know what to expect. He should have specific instruction as to the location, time, etc., of his appointment.

8. There should be a clear understanding with the parishioner about the matter of confidences and reports. What information is the pastor permitted to impart to the agency or the doctor about the counselee?

9. Whenever possible, the counselee should assist in the selection of an agency and assist in choosing alternatives; in other words, he should share in the planning of his own program and his own future.

10. A poor referral may do more harm than good. If an agency is not qualified, if it cannot accept the person because of resident restrictions, if it is not interested, etc., sending a person to it only leads to another disappointment.

11. There can be an element of rejection in all referrals. There always is an element of rejection in referral to another counselor or therapist. It may not be intended, but can be very real to the person himself. Every effort should be made to work this through so the person will understand.

12. When possible, we should arrange to follow up on a referral. How was the person received, what is his progress, how can we continue to help?

13. A good referral is based on a full knowledge of the agency. The counselor must understand its function, procedure, fee policy, etc. (See Section 26 for factors in understanding an agency.)

14. It is important to prepare the agency or the specialist for the referral and to provide them with full and accurate information about the person being referred.

FOR FURTHER GROWTH: Read from the general field of social work. Social workers know community resources and their books usually include a good discussion of referral.

RELATING THEORY TO PRACTICE: Evaluate each counseling situation with which you are working by asking three specific questions: (1) Can I provide the service this person needs the most? (2) Should he be referred? (3) If so, what agency or specialist can provide his needs the best?

26. INFORMATION ABOUT AN AGENCY

While one may not need to know all the answers to all the following questions in order to suggest an agency, these are the questions one should have in mind in considering any agency.

What is its background? What is its history? Origin? Who were the founders? What was their motivation? Is it an old agency with years of experience? Is it a new agency? How long has it existed locally?

Who sponsors the agency? Is it governmental: local, state, national? Is it privately operated? Is it religiously affiliated?

How is the agency supported? Is it supported by taxes? Fees? Endowment? Membership dues? United Fund? Religious or fraternal groups?

Who does it serve, or who can it accept for service? Are there any residence requirements? Is it limited to an age group? Racial group? Members of a lodge or church group? Those with a particular need?

What services does it offer? Do they deal only with specific problems (such as a speech clinic)? Do they meet many and varied problems (such as the Salvation Army)?

What are the expenses involved? Are services free? Is there a standard charge? A sliding scale? Can arrangements for payment be made?

How soon are services available? Is there a waiting list? If so, how long? Are any provisions for limited service provided during the waiting period? Are there exceptions in emergencies?

Where is the location? Is there public transportation? A parking problem? Is it in another community (the state capital)?

What is the training of the personnel? Are they volunteers? Social workers? Psychologists? Psychiatrists? Physicians? Teachers? Clergymen? Do they provide their own training? Is the staff represented by different disciplines? Do they maintain consultation services with other disciplines?

Does a person have to make his own appointments? What information is required? What technicalities are involved?

What are the attitudes of the staff? Are they friendly? Professional? Indifferent? Cold? Accepting? Do they have different attitudes toward different groups?

What is the opinion of other professional people about the agency? How is it accepted or evaluated by other professionals in the community? How is it regarded by Doctors, Psychiatrists, Attorneys, or Clergymen?

What are the affiliations of the agency? Is it a member of the local Council of Agencies? United Fund? Is it a member of national accrediting groups? Are its staff members of national groups such as the American Association of Social Workers, American Psychological Association, American Association of Family Counselors?

What do former clients say about the agency? Its effectiveness? Their treatment? Was their experience good?

What has been the effectiveness of the agency over the years? nationally? locally?

COMMUNITY RESOURCES: List the agencies that could give local information about community services.

	Name	Phone	Address
Council of Agencies			
United Fund (Community Chest)			
Council of Churches			
Department of Welfare			

27. PSYCHIATRIC REFERRAL

Some persons go to the pastor whose primary need is psychiatric treatment. When this is evident, he should advise them of this fact, attempt to help them recognize the need, and if need be, assist them in securing help. There are other occasions when the psychiatric problem is not recognized in the first interview, or even in the early stages of counseling, but later evidences indicate a psychiatric referral is necessary. The following factors may indicate that such a referral is advisable.

1. Irrational or unrealistic behavior or conversation, or behavior that is out of line with things as they really are.

2. Overreaction. A person is too worried, too tense, too angry, too suspicious, too hostile. (Note: this does not necessarily mean he is mentally sick. We all react this way at times, the neurotic does most of the time.) Overreaction may mean the presence of a deeper problem.

3. Evidences of extreme anxiety, either verbal or nonverbal, especially anxiety that is disabling or crippling.

4. Evidence of extreme discouragement, despondency, or depression, either verbal or nonverbal.

5. An expression of phobias or unusual fears.

6. Physical symptoms, psychosomatic complaints, inability to sleep, loss of appetite, etc.

7. Threats to do harm to themselves or others.

8. Excessive withdrawal, a tendency to retreat into one's self.

9. Excessive mood swings.

10. Excessive outbursts of anger, hostility, hatred, extreme outer social behavior.

11. Compulsive behavior, such as the necessity to wash one's hands frequently, to lock doors, etc.

12. Sudden or extreme changes in behavior patterns.
13. Descriptions of deviant sexual behavior.
14. Excessive use of alcohol or drugs.
15. Excessive suspicion, feeling that others are plotting against one, others are watching one, etc.
16. Grandiose ideas of one's own importance.
17. Periods of confusion, no related theme to conversation.
18. Hearing voices, seeing visions, receiving messages.
19. A lack of sensitivity, having no feeling of regret or remorse about definite misbehavior, a lack of conscience.
20. Tangential references to subjects as if they were being directly discussed.
21. A sense of alienation and a lack of response.
22. Evidence that a person is in apparent need of drugs.

FOR FURTHER STUDY: Read books listed in the Bibliography under Psychiatry, Mental Health, and Abnormal Psychology.

COMMUNITY RESOURCES: List the mental health resources.

Name	Phone	Address
Mental Health Association		
Mental Health Clinic		
Mental Health and Mental Retardation Center		
Psychiatrists		

28. THE COUNSELOR AND THE PHYSICIAN

Most people who go to a pastor or a pastoral counseling center are in reasonably good health. Some may also be under the care of a physician. Some are referred by physicians. The person's physical condition may or may not be an influential factor in the problems he is discussing with the pastor. When a person goes to a pastor for counseling, the pastor should secure permission to consult with his physician if necessary. The following guidelines should be followed.

1. The pastor should inform the counselee that he needs to consult with the physician when a counselee is on medication such as tranquilizers, antidepressants, or other drugs that would affect his moods, effectiveness, or general well-being. It is important for the pastor to know why such medication was prescribed. When the coun-

selee manifests behavior which would be influential in the treatment of his physical ills, the pastor should also provide this information to his doctor--if the physician is desirous of receiving such information.

2. When a counselee complains of physical symptoms, such as insomnia, headaches, backaches, fatigue, or others, the pastor should insist on a medical examination and evaluation.

3. When the pastor feels that a counselee, who is also under the care of a doctor, needs psychiatric treatment, he should consult with the doctor about what he would prefer to be done and, if a psychiatrist is indicated, which one he would prefer.

The doctor and the pastor overlap in the field of emotions. Fear, anxiety, guilt, tension all have physical accompaniments. In turn, physical ills create emotional concerns. The doctor focuses on the illness, the disease, and the medication and treatment that is necessary. In doing so, he usually recognizes he must consider the patient as a whole. The pastor begins with the patient as a whole and is concerned not with the diagnosis and treatment of the physical illness, but with the person's reaction to it, what it means to him, how he may cope with it, etc.

FOR FURTHER STUDY: Read some of the recent material on psychosomatic medicine.

COMMUNITY RESOURCES: Medical Association Doctors

_____

_____

_____

_____

_____

29. PASTORAL COUNSELING IN THE HOSPITAL

The pastor in the parish calls regularly on his parishioners who are ill. Such calls may lead to counseling, or they may not. A person who is seeing a pastoral counselor at a counseling center may become ill and request the counselor to call on him. The first concern at such a time is for the patient to get well. It usually is wise to delay counseling until the person has recovered and, while he is ill, to confine oneself to pastoral care. There may be occasions when concerns of a counseling nature have a bearing on the recovery. Then the pastor works in close collaboration with the patient's physician, observing all the principles of pastoral care listed below.

When ministering in a hospital there are certain rules and principles to observe.

1. The physician is in charge of the sickroom. What you do, do in conjunction with the physician's requests and requirements.

2. Be aware of hospital administrative requirements, visiting hours, fire regulations, etc.

3. Get what information you can about the patient and his condition before you make the call. Get the information from the proper sources--the doctor, the nurse, the family. Do not ask the nurse for information she is not permitted to give.

4. Prepare yourself in mind and spirit before entering the room. Recall any previous contacts with the patient.

5. Be careful to note all "No Visitors" or other signs that may have been posted. The doctor has placed them there for a purpose. They do not necessarily mean that a pastor cannot call. They do mean he should be aware of their reasons for being there.

6. If the door is closed, if the light that summons a nurse is on in the hall, ask a nurse if it is all right to enter. Never embarrass a patient.

7. Recognize the importance of such mechanical things as where you sit or stand. Do not jar or sit on the bed. Never stand or sit with a bright light (sun, a lamp) behind you. Never sit where the patient has to lean on one elbow, or strain to see you.

8. Shake hands if the patient offers first. At the church you make the first move. In the hospital the patient does.

9. Excuse yourself when the doctor is present, unless he asks you to stay. Excuse yourself when a meal is being served. Food and rest are important in convalescence. Food is not good when it is cold. Excuse yourself when other visitors are present. A hospital room is no place for a crowd. There are exceptions when these rules do not apply, but in the main they should be observed.

10. Adapt to the mood of the patient. It is well to be slightly on the cheerful side, but don't try to be funny. Don't carry "emotional germs" from one room to another. If one call has been discouraging, pause for awhile before making the next one.

11. Don't reveal negative emotional feelings as a result of sights, sounds, odors, etc. Patients are self-conscious about such matters.

12. Maintain an attitude of quiet, peace, and confidence. Attitudes are contagious. If you are relaxed, quiet, and calm, the patient will be helped to be relaxed and quiet.

13. Speak in a natural tone of voice. Do not whisper, and do not speak too loudly. Avoid the "holy whine." Do not speak to others in the room assuming the patient will not hear--sometimes he does.

14. Don't give medical advice or use medical terms. This is the doctor's field. Don't discuss other people's illnesses, or your own. Don't get maneuvered into discussing one doctor against another. Don't discuss the medical fees, except as you may discuss the patient's concern about them. The validity of a fee is between the patient and the doctor.

15. Don't talk too much. Listen more than you talk. Give the patient every opportunity to express his feelings and concerns.

16. Do not argue, probe, or condemn. Always maintain the good will of the patient when possible. In counseling we may need to confront a counselee and even in convalescence it may be indicated. During early stages of illness, it is not. The pastor needs convictions about race, economic justice, war, and peace, but the sick room is usually not the place to argue them. Never unduly excite or agitate a patient.

17. Don't stay too long. Never tire a patient. If the patient appears restless, if his interest lags, excuse yourself. Do not give the impression you are in a hurry. It implies a lack of concern to the patient.

18. Do not call once and then forget the patient. Pastoral calls during convalescence can be valuable. Follow up on all calls.

19. Do not wake a patient unless the nurse indicates that the patient has had adequate rest. Call again when the patient is awake.

20. When the patient is sleeping or is not in the room, or for any reason is unavailable, leave a note expressing your interest. This in itself can be supportive.

21. Do not call when you are sick. A note or card can express your interest.

22. Utilize religious resources such as prayer and scripture whenever the patient requests it or when it seems indicated by the nature of the situation. Keep both the reading of scripture and the use of prayer brief. Scriptures should be selected that are supportive in nature, that stress reassurance, forgiveness, faith, and love. Prayer should be in the words and thought patterns of the patient's age and religious background. A written passage or printed prayer left with a patient may be read and reread when the pastor is not present. Some excellent pastoral aid materials are available for this purpose. The use of religious resources should be natural and sincere.

23. It may be helpful at times, at the doctor's request and with his help, to assist the patient in understanding the nature of his illness.

24. Don't neglect the patient's family. They too need a ministry. In helping them, you also help the patient and the doctor.

FOR FURTHER STUDY: Read any general books on pastoral care, also some that have been written on a hospital ministry as such.

COMMUNITY RESOURCES: List hospital personnel.

	Name	Phone	Hospital
Hospital Chaplains	_____	_____	_____
Hospital Administrators	_____	_____	_____

30. LEGAL MATTERS

Some persons who go to a pastor have problems of a legal nature. They may raise questions about legal matters such as divorce laws, child support, adoption, property rights, bail, zoning, etc. Certain guidelines should determine procedures when legal matters are an issue.

1. The pastor does not attempt to give legal advice or counsel. Even when he thinks he knows the law, there may be technicalities or procedures with which he is not familiar. When it is important for him to know what legal steps are available, he should secure the information from an attorney. When a counselee must take legal actions, he must secure adequate legal counsel.

2. It should be remembered that laws vary from state to state; laws change from year to year; laws are interpreted differently by different judges. Hearsay, memory, or previous experience can be very misleading. Where legal matters are involved, the pastor should get the facts and procedures from the proper sources.

3. Lawyers, like preachers and psychiatrists, have different personalities and interests. Lawyers take several different attitudes toward divorce. Some welcome counseling for a couple before divorce; some discourage it. In recommending an attorney for a person or a family, it is important to know his attitudes, as well as his legal background and experience.

4. Recognize that a lawyer practices under definite and specific patterns and codes of ethics. He respects confidences, he cannot receive money from his client's opponent, he attempts to settle matters out of court when it is to his client's interest. He does not advertise or solicit clients, etc.

5. Attorneys take different attitudes toward counseling as such. The typical country lawyer of a generation ago gave his clients all sorts of counsel about personal and family matters as well as legal matters. Some lawyers still state that a large percentage of their discussion with their clients deals with matters that are not strictly legal matters. Law schools are adding psychological and psychiatric factors to their programs of instruction. The general pattern, however, is that the lawyer is a specialist in "legal" matters as such.

6. The lawyer, like the psychiatrist, the social worker, and the clergyman, has a symbolic role. Because he is a lawyer, people see him in a particular frame of reference. This varies with the client's background and previous experience with the legal profession. Clients usually expect a lawyer to take the lead, seek pertinent facts and information, and provide a solution to their problems.

7. Lawyers also see themselves in certain patterns. To quote from Harrop Freeman:

"He (the lawyer) represents the 'law' or authority; he is an authority figure. He has community powers which are at his call. His diploma and bar admission guarantee his qualifications. His approach is 'logical' or 'reasonable' rather than 'moral' or 'religious' and he does not require people to appear only when they are 'sick' or 'patients.' His time is for sale to those who will pay. . . . The lawyer must remain aware that he is a legal specialist and must represent the social interest in upholding the legal system as well as meet the client expectations."*

We would add to this that lawyers see themselves as a part of an adversary system, which governs their relationship to their client and to those with whom the client is having difficulty.

8. The legal aid society is a nonprofit, charitable organization established "to secure the rendering of legal aid service and counsel gratuitously to those persons of the community who appear worthy thereof and who by reason of financial circumstances are unable to pay for the same." It considers cases primarily of a civil nature.

9. The American Bar Association has a committee on legal aid (civil cases) and defender services (criminal cases) for the poor or those unable to secure legal counsel. The local chapter will offer assistance in securing legal counsel for those unable to hire an attorney, through what is called "Lawyer Referral Services." When a person has no legal counsel and the issue is brought to the court, the court assigns an attorney.

COMMUNITY RESOURCES: List legal resources.

	Name	Phone	Address
Bar Association	_____	_____	_____
Legal Aid	_____	_____	_____
Attorneys	_____	_____	_____
	_____	_____	_____
	_____	_____	_____

31. CONFIDENTIAL INFORMATION AND PRIVILEGED COMMUNICATION

All successful counseling (pastoral or otherwise) is based on the premise that this is a confidential relationship. Unless the counselee feels that the counselor will hold all information given him in complete trust, no effective results can be expected. This is a covenant relationship that must not be violated.

Every person who comes to a pastor for help should be assured that he will be treated professionally and that all information about him will be handled confidentially.

The following guidelines should be followed closely:

1. Never discuss a case no matter how interesting it could be as a matter of conversation or gossip. Even if the person might never know, others who hear it may feel that the pastor does not respect confidences.

*Legal Interviewing and Counseling (West, 1964), pp. 6-7.

2. Never use a case as an illustration in a public address or sermon.

3. When a referral is indicated, and a person is sent to a psychiatrist, social worker, physician, social agency, or anyone else, his permission should be secured to discuss the situation with the specialist. In a counseling center the person is usually asked to sign a release so that information (professional communication) can be provided to the specialist or agency. When he is aware that it is for his own good, he is usually willing to grant such permission.

4. When a person is so out of touch with reality that such permission might not be secured, or if the person is a danger to himself or others, a decision must be made, sometimes in consultation with his family. There may be occasions where information is given without receiving the person's permission.

5. If one is dealing with a minor, or someone in a dependent role with a parent or guardian, or a student who is seriously ill, one may need to notify his parents, family physician, guardian, school authorities, or the one most responsible for the minor's welfare. When one does so, in most cases, he should inform the person that he is doing so and why. He should not disclose the details of the problem, but rather that the person needs help.

6. One should not include in any written records material that would be embarrassing or harmful to the person. Records can be subpoenaed.

The legal status of "privileged communication" for clergymen is very confused, varies from state to state, and is in a continual state of transition. There is no federal legislation on privileged communication of the clergy. Thirty-seven states have statutes which usually stipulate that information granted to clergymen is "privileged" if it is "penitential in character and made to him in his professional character in confidence while seeking religious or spiritual advice, aid, or comfort."* States or territories which do not have specific laws that apply follow common-law practice, which means that "privileged communication" may or may not be granted, depending upon the decision of the judges and attorneys involved.

Wayne Oates speaks of a "covenant of communication." This, he says, is "more than a promise not to tell anything the person has said, which may or may not be a wise thing to promise. A covenant of communication consists of a _mutual_ understanding that both the counselor and counselee will consult with each other before either of them discusses their conversation with anyone else.**

The minister is in a somewhat different position from other counselors in that he also hears confessions. This is true whether he is in a liturgical church or not. It may be quite informal and absolution may not be pronounced, but it is spiritual confession, nonetheless. Speaking of this "confessional" information, Dr. Oates says, "These are things which people literally tell to God in our presence as helpers and encouragers. Therefore, they are not things that really are ours to tell."***

*Statute of the State of Minnesota. Quoted in The Right to Silence, by W. H. Tiemann (John Knox, 1964), p. 92.

**Protestant Pastoral Counseling (Westminster Press, 1967), p. 175.

***Wayne Oates, An Introduction to Pastoral Counseling (Broadman Press, 1959), p. 92.

RELATING THEORY TO PRACTICE: Reflect on any recent counseling experiences and ask yourself if any have been discussed in private conversation. Review all sermon notes, and notes from public speeches that will be used again and delete any references to information that was learned in a confidential relationship.

32. SOME PROBLEMS IN COUNSELING

Frequently problems arise in counseling that interrupt or prevent progress toward desired goals. Some seem to be paradoxical in nature, such as the counselee who comes for help but resists it; some are external, not created either by the pastor or counselee, such as interruptions or distractions. Some of the more common problems are:

Silence and Pauses. Silence and long pauses in the conversation may be sources of embarrassment and tension for both counselor and counselee. The silence may be due to many reasons. The counselee may be too embarrassed to continue the story; he may be resisting the necessity of doing so; he may be so moved emotionally that he is afraid his voice will break; he may be attempting to determine what he should say next; he may be waiting for the counselor to speak, he may be trying to get up enough nerve to discuss a new topic; he may be thinking over what he has said; he may not know what is expected of him; he may be so discouraged he sees no point in talking; he may be tired from emotional strain and resting--any one, or a combination, of such factors can cause a pause in the conversation.

The counselor should remember that the silent time usually seems longer than it is.

It is a courtesy and a help with some persons just to sit in silence so they do not have to speak. If the period of silence itself becomes a strain, the counselor should assist the counselee by asking a question or suggesting another area of discussion. Maybe he should ask, "Why the silence?"

Resistance. The counselor should expect some resistance in counseling. It is probably inevitable. Resistance, like silence, may be due to many things--embarrassment, lack of trust in the confidential relationship, the fear of change (even for the better), the methods of the counselor, too much probing, curiosity, moralizing, overprotection, etc.

When resistance occurs, it should be seen as a clue to the counselee's needs and as a part of his problem. It should also be seen as a signal to evaluate one's methods and the nature of the transference or countertransference that is present. (See Section 37.)

When resistance can be evaluated and interpreted, it can be a means of real growth.

Setbacks. A counselor should expect an occasional setback. This may be due to outside influences, it may be a result of the process itself. A client may be so relieved by his initial verbalizing of a problem that he expects everything to be correspondingly better. When old problems return, he feels he has not gained any ground and may be unduly discouraged. Some may regress in order to secure more attention or to seek a firmer base from which to grow.

Severe regression may indicate a referral. Normal or mild setbacks are taken in stride, the counselee is accepted and supported during the setbacks and encouraged to continue.

Interruptions and Distractions. At its best, counseling takes place free of interruptions and distractions. In actuality, both occur. This is true whether there be one interview or a series of interviews.

Interruptions by telephone, a knock at the door, etc., may be disconcerting but need not be serious. Some counselors have found that such interruptions even have value. They help the counselee realize that others have problems too. The obvious solution is to deal with the cause of the interruption and get back to the task at hand. If a counselor knows an interruption, such as a phone call, is likely to occur, he should inform the counselee of this fact before the hour begins.

Interruptions may occur in a series of interviews due to vacations, illness, work demands, etc., on the part of either counselee or counselor. These too can be turned to advantage. An interruption can give the person a chance to go on his own for a week and to find new confidence in being able to do so. One can utilize the time to do free writing (see Section 46) and thus retain the pattern of focusing on the problem and then going on about one's responsibilites.

Distractions such as sounds, sights, etc., should be anticipated in advance. A counselor's room should not be cluttered, disordered, etc. When distractions do occur, unless they are so intense as to make concentration impossible, they should be ignored. On occasion the counselor may want to find out why a person is bothered by a certain distraction.

Time Limits. Most counseling interviews last about one hour. There is nothing sacred about a fifty-minute hour. Experience has seemed to indicate most problems require this much time; however, it may be that on other occasions less time is appropriate and correct.

If a problem has been resolved, if a person is too discouraged to talk further, if a counselee should request that he be permitted to stop sooner, or if it seems that one's goals have been attained in less time, one should not force the counselee to fill out a full hour.

If more time is needed, one should not hesitate to continue, within limits. If a great deal more time is needed, it is usually better to return the next day or in a few days than to extend a session indefinitely. If a person is leaving town, or for any reason will be unavailable, it may indicate more time must be given.

It is well that the counselee know at the beginning of the session what the terminal time will be, then he will be prepared for it.

If a person feels that he needs more time but the counselor has another appointment, it is usually advisable to inform the person of the situation and arrange another meeting--unless his problem is so crucial it must be continued at that time. In this case, the pastor should notify the counselee who is waiting for his session so he will understand the delay. It may help both counselees to know that others have problems too. In this case the counselor must evaluate which counselee could accept the delay with the least amount of tension. It may be that the person in his office should be the one to wait.

It is well to inform a counselee at the beginning of his sessions of the above guidelines.

FOR FURTHER STUDY: Read widely in the field of general counseling.

RELATING THEORY TO PRACTICE: Review any recent counseling situations. If you feel that certain problems are recurring frequently, discuss the situation with a consultant (pychiatrist, psychologist, or pastor).

33. THOSE WHO COME TO THE PASTOR UNWILLINGLY

Not everyone who goes to a pastor or counseling center goes because he wants to. Some go because they were pressured, nagged, forced, or required to go. When this is the case, the person is naturally resistant, defensive, angry, and uncoop- erative. Sometimes what appears to be resistance may not actually be that. The person really is desirous of working on his problem but gives a different impression. There are other situations when the resistance is real but not strong, and can soon be resolved. Even when the person does resist the counselor, it does not mean the person cannot be helped; it does mean certain guidelines should be followed.

1. Little will be accomplished until these negative, resistant emotions are faced and dealt with.

2. One way of dealing with these emotions is to reflect the feelings that are expressed by the person. This often communicates to the person that the counselor understands.

3. Another method is to interpret frankly to the person that one understands how he feels and recognizes that his feelings are natural and to be expected.

4. It is important to interpret and define the counseling procedure so that the counselee will understand that the counselor is not on anyone's side. His purpose is to help.

5. When a person has expressed his resentment and resistance and finds he is still accepted and will not be judged or preached to, he may enter into the coun- seling process with real appreciation and cooperation.

RELATING THEORY TO PRACTICE: Evaluate your recent counseling interviews. How many counselees came willingly? reluctantly? unwillingly? What were your reactions to their attitudes? What methods did you use to reduce their resistance?

34. SEMANTICS AND COMMUNICATION

There are many forms of communication between persons, both verbal and non-verbal. Not only the words one uses, but the tone of one's voice, the actions of the body, the expression on one's face, the look in one's eyes are means of communication.

Language, however, is one of the main means by which people communicate. Communication is one of man's basic psychological needs. Communication only takes place when speaker and hearer understand each other. Semantics is defined as the "science of meanings." This has great importance in pastoral counseling.

Many emotional disorders are a result of the failure of people to find common meaning between themselves, husband and wife, parent and child, employer and employee. Many people who seek counseling are having trouble in communicating with "significant others" in their lives.

1. Some who come for counseling may have no one else with whom they can really communicate, at the moment, except the counselor.

2. Communication only takes place between counselor and counselee when they use words in the same way. Words in the American language have many meanings and are used by different subcultures in different ways.

3. Everyone responds to words in the light of his own background and experience. Words like "love," "father," "mother," "guilt," and "sin" are emotionally loaded words and mean different things to different people, or they have multiple meanings. Meanings are not in words but in persons.

4. Technical words, either theological or psychological, should usually be avoided. They only have full meaning to the student or the specialists.

5. Educated persons sometimes use vocabulary that is very confusing to children, to the elderly, or to the high school dropout. One should not "talk down" to people, but speak in terms they understand. It takes great wisdom to speak simply.

6. One should only use language in which he can converse with confidence and comfort. The pastor who tries to talk in the current language of the teen-ager, or to swear with the man of the world only makes himself look foolish.

7. People under stress listen more intensely than do people in casual conversation. They often attach more meaning to words or phrases than the counselor intends, or they selectively block words that are a threat. It isn't what we say that is important; it is what the person thinks he hears. When there is doubt about the counselees getting the meaning in communication, he should be asked to tell what he has heard.

8. Some people, because of biases, prejudices, or emotional blocks, only hear portions of what is said. By the "power of selective inattention" they tune out what they do not want to hear.

9. Communication between counselor and counselee requires occasional "feedback," so each person knows whether he is being understood.

10. Talking and communicating are two different things. People may be talk-

ing to each other but not communicating at all. One of the counselor's chief tasks in family counseling is to help people communicate better and to keep the channels of communication open and controlled. One of the advantages of Virginia Satir's concept of Conjoint Family Therapy is that it enables the counselor to observe the communication that is taking place in the family and, on occasion, to clarify it.

A simple procedure to follow when two people seem to be having difficulty communicating is to ask each to explain what the other has said and what he meant.

11. Providing a means and an opportunity for genuine communication about life's deepest needs and problems is itself a service. Helping people to communicate with others is equally valuable.

12. Take note of all nonverbal "signs" that seem to have meaning on the part of the counselee and make a record of them. (See Section 6.)

RELATING THEORY TO PRACTICE: Review any recent counseling situations. Note whether or not you felt communication was taking place. Study the vocabulary that was used. Note any words you did not understand, or any words you may have used that the counselee did not understand.

35. THE MIDDLE PHASES OF EXTENDED COUNSELING

Some of the people who go to a pastor or a counseling center can be helped by brief or short-term counseling. Some need extended counseling over a longer period of time. During the middle phases of longer counseling programs, certain goals and procedures should be kept in mind.

Goals of Counseling

The goals of long-term counseling are usually more inclusive and extensive than other forms of counseling or pastoral care. Goals vary with the needs of the person. What might be a goal with one person may not be with another. The degree to which goals can be attained varies with the nature and complexity of the problems, the motivation of the counselee, and the skill of the counselor, as well as other variables. It should be pointed out these goals are just that. They are directions in which one is moving, and no one attains them all completely.

1. An increasing degree of self-understanding and self-acceptance. (See Section 16, "Insight Counseling.") This would include a knowledge of one's past, the reasons for one's behavior, an awareness of one's strengths and weaknesses and the ability to accept both, without undue pride on the one hand or self-pity on the other.

2. Reasonable, realistic goals for the future that contain a real challenge,

but are based on realistic thinking and planning, without grandiose schemes that are impossible to attain or low standards that are based on a fear of failure. Personal plans and ambitions that will result in growth and achievement but contain the "courage of imperfection."

3. An increasing degree of self-confidence and self-esteem, so that one can "love his neighbors as himself" in a wholesome way.

4. Improved interpersonal relations, free from the crippling effects of dependency or uncontrolled hostility. An increasing capacity to understand, to accept other people's imperfections, to love and be loved, and to maintain lasting relationships. "Now abideth faith, hope and love, . . . but the greatest of these is love." (1 Corinthians 13:13)

5. The development and use of tension-reducing techniques, or high-level skills of adjustment, are related to the individual's interests, abilities, and maturity.

6. A realistic outlook on life that recognizes that every one has problems, tensions, and disappointments so these things do not come as too much of a surprise or threat.

7. An increasing sense of vocation and purpose. Sigmund Freud said the healthy person is able to find meaning in work. This may be in vocation or avocation or both.

8. An increasing willingness to serve, to develop what Adler called "social interest," and to feel that one has a contribution to make. "He that would save his life must lost it." (Matthew 16:25)

9. A willingness to accept responsibility without excuse or complaining.

10. A capacity to relax, to play, to enjoy oneself. Tension and relaxation are incompatible. "You will break the bow if you keep it always stretched." An increasing sense of humor, the ability to see the ludicrous and the funny things in life and, on occasion, to laugh at oneself.

11. A deeper and growing awareness that one is a child of God and a realization of the guiding and sustaining power that comes through faith and trust. The "basic trust" of which Erikson speaks is a pastor's ultimate goal. It may be very small and tentative but it can grow. "If you have faith as a grain of a mustard seed . . ." (Matthew 17:20).

Procedures and Emphases in the Middle Phases of Counseling

Bearing in mind the above, the following methodological procedures should be considered.

1. The counselor should look for predominant themes that are repeated, that are characteristic of a person's thoughts and behavior.

2. The counselor should maintain a tentative evaluation that is reevaluated as new data is presented and new experiences are discussed.

3. There may be occasions when it is well to clarify goals with the counselee to assure better understanding of the counseling process.

4. The counselor usually can be more active in making interpretations, suggestions, etc., during the middle phases than in the early phases when he is at-

tempting to establish a relationship and gain rapport, or in the latter stages when it is up to the counselee to do so.

5. The counselor must be more alert for transference in the middle phases of long-term counseling than one would expect in short-term counseling.

6. The counselor should usually reenforce all positive, healthy moves on the part of the counselee. This would be determined by the familial and social context of the counseling.

7. The counselor should be aware that the goals listed above are never attained perfectly, that their growth should be slow and gradual, and that there are, however, occasional sudden flashes of insight. There also may be plateaus and setbacks, as well as advances, and these may be essential in preparing the ground for further advances. The counselor needs to recognize the need for patience and keep up the motivation both for himself and for the counselee.

8. Prepare the counselee for the completion of counseling when termination is indicated. (See Section 36, "Termination of Counseling.")

RELATING THEORY TO PRACTICE: Check every extended counseling situation once a month. Check the following questions: Are there recurring themes? What progress has been made? Is a referral indicated? What are your continuing goals?

36. TERMINATION OF COUNSELING

While it is important that counseling have a good beginning, it is equally important that it have a good conclusion. Termination of counseling may be indicated when the counselee feels the problem has been successfully resolved. Termination may be indicated when the counselor feels the problem or problems have been successfully resolved. Hopefully these will coincide, but not always. Termination may be indicated when the counselee and the counselor recognize that the problems still exist (and may continue to exist) but the counselee has sufficient insight and strengths to cope with them. Termination may be indicated when the counselee or the counselor is dissatisfied with the progress and feels that continued efforts will not prove profitable. Termination may be necessary when the counselee moves away, changes employment, goes away to school or into the service, or for any reason is not available for continued counseling. Termination may be indicated when to go further would require such extensive therapy that the effort involved would not be justified by the results.

The following considerations should be kept in mind for termination of cases.

1. It is well at the beginning of counseling to set an evaluation point after

four to six interviews, at which time an evaluation can be made and a decision reached as to whether counseling has been complete, there is a need to refer or to continue. This gives a natural and agreed-upon point at which to discuss the issue.

2. If the counselee feels the problem has been resolved, but the counselor feels other problems exist that need to be faced, the counselor should indicate this fact and suggest the possibility of continued counseling. If the counselee still feels it unnecessary, he may be asked to check back with the counselor once more for an evaluation, or may be informed that he can always return if he desires.

3. If the counselor feels the problems have been resolved, but the counselee wishes to prolong the relationship, the whole situation should be evaluated to determine whether there are more problems than the counselor had recognized (or wished to recognize), or whether the counselee--because of dependency feelings or other secondary gains--is unnecessarily prolonging the experience. If so, the procedure would be as in (2) above.

4. Long-term counseling cases should be periodically evaluated with a supervisor to determine whether there is transference, countertransference, or any other factor that is prolonging the procedures unnecessarily.

5. When a counselee or a counselor feels that progress is unsatisfactory, or that progress is not being made and that the problems still exist, every effort should be made either to transfer the counselee to another counselor, or to refer him to another agency in the community.

6. When it is necessary to terminate a relationship because a counselee is leaving the community, the counselor should reinforce the gains that have been made, prepare the counselee for what problems he may be expected to face, suggest to him that he find further counseling in the new community if the problems are rather difficult. There may be occasions when the pastor will help to locate another counselor by mail or phone.

7. When the counselor anticipates that termination is approaching, he should prepare the counselee by suggesting that in one more session or so they should be able to complete the process, or that counseling will no longer be necessary.

8. In the closing stages of counseling one may prepare for termination by going from one session a week to one every two weeks, or even once a month. This gives the counselee a chance to gain confidence by going on his own, but also to have a chance to continue if he feels a need.

9. Termination, for whatever reason, should be positive but realistic. The counselee should be made to feel--even if he is disappointed in the results--that it was significant for him to make the effort. He should recognize, no matter how successful counseling has been, that other problems may present themselves, but he has had the experience of facing issues and he can return to counseling if need be.

RELATING THEORY TO PRACTICE: Reevaluate all recent counseling situations in light of the following questions: Was termination premature? Were promises made for follow-up? For possible renewal of counseling?

37. TRANSFERENCE AND COUNTERTRANSFERENCE

Anyone who is familiar with psychoanalytic literature is aware of the phenomenon known as transference and countertransference. One of the simplest definitions of transference is that the patient "reacts to the therapist as though he were a figure of the past." It means attributing to another person feelings, qualities, attitudes, or ideas which do not necessarily belong to him, but may in fact be reasonable or present. It is the unconscious transfer to the counselor of feelings that a person originally had, or wished he had had, with key figures in earlier life. Others, who do not accept the psychoanalytic position, describe it in different terms but the facts are the same. The pastoral counselor must be aware of this fact. Some factors to consider are as follows.

1. Transference takes place all the time, not only in counseling. Transference is more likely to occur there, because of the personal, intensive, often intimate nature of counseling. It is also more likely to occur here because there is not the opportunity for feelings to be verified in experience.

2. Transference may be negative or positive, erotic or hostile. It may express feelings once greatly enjoyed, greatly missed, or greatly feared. It may include love, hate, competition, attraction, hostility--all depending on how the person reacted to the transference figure in early life.

3. The psychoanalytically oriented psychiatrist or psychologist utilizes transference. It is intentionally induced by the therapist, so that the patient can relive and release experiences in relationship with the therapist. The transference state is then dissolved for more mature adjustment. The pastor does not induce or use transference in the same way. He should be aware of it and be able at times to interpret it.

4. The fact that a pastor is a father figure in many people's eyes may facilitate transference. Howard Clinebell says the pastor is a "religious transference figure." Because of his symbolic role, his association with the church, the pastor stirs up a variety of early-life feelings and associations about religion, faith, right and wrong, the church, God, judgment, guilt, hope, parents, etc.

5. When a pastor recognizes that strong transference feelings exist, he should clarify for the person just what is happening, and why. Mild transference feelings are probably best left undiscussed. When the transference is strong or continued, a referral may be indicated.

6. Frequent appointments and long-term counseling increase the possibility of transference. In occasional appointments or short-term counseling it is not as likely to occur.

7. Complete permissiveness, much silence, and expressions of affection are likely to increase the possibility of transference, while a consistent professional pastoral manner decreases the likelihood of transference.

8. Group counseling can also produce transference. The person transfers to the group or the leader feelings he had toward families or groups he may have had, or hoped for.

Countertransference, as the term implies, refers to the feelings the counselor

90

may also have toward counselees. Some consider all of a counselor's reactions as countertransference, others include only a counselor's unconscious reaction to the counselee's transference feelings.

Dr. Orr, speaking of the counselor says, "He differs from the client, however, in being more aware of his needs and impulses, having them under greater self-observation and conscious control and, above all, knowing that they must find gratification in other relationships than those with clients."*

1. Countertransference, like transference, can be positive or negative.

2. It is natural to like or dislike a person. If a counselor's feelings about a counselee become intense, it can create a problem. To see a woman as sexually attractive is one thing; to exploit that feeling or act upon it is another. Being disappointed in a person's progress is one thing, being angry with him for not progressing is another.

3. Clues to the possible presence of countertransference: A counselor feels tired, bored, is late for an appointment; he becomes tense or angry, or feels uncomfortable or uneasy with a certain counselee; he becomes overprotective, overconcerned, overly reassuring or optimistic, or begins to spend excessive amounts of time with one counselee; or he feels he is responding differently to one counselee than to others, etc.

4. When one becomes aware of the presence of countertransference and realizes that it is blocking the progress of counseling, he needs to reassess his approach and to evaluate his own feelings. If countertransference still persists, he should consult a counselor himself to clarify his own feelings. It may mean the person should be seen by another counselor.

FOR FURTHER STUDY: Read the literature in the Bibliography particularly relating to depth psychology and psychoanalysis.

RELATING THEORY TO PRACTICE: Evaluate all counseling cases for the presence of transference, either negative or positive. When you feel that strong transference or countertransference feelings are present, check with a consultant.

38. THE TEACHING FUNCTION OF PASTORAL COUNSELING

Jesus was frequently referred to as Master or Teacher, though most of his teaching was informal in nature and frequently done on a one-to-one basis--for example, his conversations with Nicodemus, the woman at the well, Mary and Martha, James and John, etc.

There are occasions when those who come for pastoral counseling need information or instruction. On such occasions the pastor is an educator though his class may consist of only one, two, or a small group. Such instruction has been

*D. W. Orr, Professional Counseling on Human Behavior (Franklin Watts, 1965), p. 111.

referred to as "pastoral teaching," or "educational therapy," or "educational pastoral counseling."

1. The pastor is expected to be an authority in such areas as doctrine or theology, biblical interpretation, ethics and morals, denominational or ecclesiastical polity, and in matters not specifically religious. Some persons may want information about what have been called "the common ventures of everyday life"--how to adopt a child, how to discipline one's children, how to prepare for college, etc.

2. Some educational counseling is done in response to specific questions. What does the Bible teach about marriage? What does one have to do to become a minister? What is the position of the church on race problems?

3. It is imperative that the pastor have a good general education and a good theological education, and that he continually be learning and expanding his knowledge.

4. It is not necessary that the pastor can or should have information about everything. This is not only impossible but ridiculous. He should know the sources of information and not hesitate to say he does not know when he doesn't have the information.

5. It is a basic principle of all education that one learns most effectively when he is seeking information to resolve a certain problem or meet a specific need.

6. Not all educational counseling need be problem-centered. It may be growth-centered. Francis P. Robinson, in his book Principles and Procedures in Student Counseling, speaks of "Higher Level Skills of Adjustment." His thesis is that there are many people who are not neurotic, delinquent, or maladjusted who could be operating at a much higher level of adjustment and service if they had the guidance and information to do so. This may well be one of the counseling emphases of the future.

7. Some persons need information and do not realize it. In this case they need to be made aware that further information would be helpful.

8. One should be aware that a request for information may or may not be a person's primary need. One should also inquire why the person desires the information and allow plenty of time for an expression of feelings to be sure this is the major factor.

9. A request for information should usually be honored. It may be that the counselor feels that other factors are equally or more significant; yet the information should also be provided either personally or by reference to other material. (See Section 45, "Bibliotherapy.")

10. Giving information can be very satisfying to the counselor. Here is a chance to do something specific, to demonstrate his knowledge. He should be cautious that he does not shut off the expression of feeling on the part of the counselee preventing further discussion or further questions, or that he gives far more information than is needed or appropriate.

11. Giving instruction in the interview, like in the classroom, must be adapted to the occasion and the person. Begin where the pupil (counselee) is, use language he understands, proceed at his pace.

12. Educational counseling should be seen as a joint quest, not as an authority giving answers, or a professor conducting an examination, but as two people seeking a deeper and fuller understanding.

FOR FURTHER STUDY: All reading in the field of Christian thought, biblical interpretation, or religious resources will be helpful here.

FOR PERSONAL GROWTH: Write out those aspects of the Christian faith which you feel are particularly therapeutic, challenging, and strengthening.

COMMUNITY RESOURCES: List any pastors, professors, or others you think would be helpful in providing religious guidance to particular groups of particular subjects.

Name	Phone	Address
_____	_____	_____
_____	_____	_____
_____	_____	_____

PASTORAL AID MATERIALS: List books that could be loaned to deepen a counselee's understanding of the Christian faith.

_____
_____
_____
_____

39. RELIGIOUS RESOURCES

Howard Clinebell said the pastoral counselor "should strive to become an expert in spiritual growth--knowing how to stimulate it and how to help remove the things that block it." He continues:
"Pastoral counseling has a quality of uniqueness about it which stems
from regarding spiritual growth as an essential objective in counseling.
This goal should be explicit in the pastor's mind, although it may or
may not be discussed, in a particular counseling relationship."*
For centuries religious resources such as prayer and Scripture, religious convictions, beliefs, and faith have been a source of reassurance, guidance, strength, and growth.

*Basic Types of Pastoral Counseling (Abingdon Press, 1966), pp. 50, 52.

There is an increasing awareness on the part of many in the secular disciplines of the value of religious beliefs and practices. Carl Jung, noted European psycho-analyst, said, "Among all my patients in the second half of life--that is to say, over thirty-five--there has not been one whose problem in the last resort was not that of finding a religious outlook on life. It is safe to say that every one of them feel ill because he had lost touch with that which the living religions of every age have given to their followers, and none of them has been healed who did not regain his religious outlook."*

Erik Erikson, noted American psychologist says, "For the first component of a healthy personality I nominate a sense of basic trust. . . . The psychopathologist cannot avoid observing that there are millions of people who cannot really afford to be without religion, and whose pride in not having it is that much whistling in the dark. . . . Whosoever claims that he does not need religion must derive such basic faith from elsewhere."**

1. People who go to a pastor, a church, or a pastoral counseling center do so because it has a religious affiliation and orientation. They may be troubled by doubt, they may be suffering from guilt, they may have religious questions, they may have a wistful longing for something which they cannot quite express. These feelings may or may not be expressed in religious terms.

2. There may be some who could and should be supported or sustained by religious resources. Some are definitely seeking such assistance. They may ask for a prayer or for guidance from Scripture. Others may wish for such an expression but feel too shy or embarrassed to ask. Many have such limited background of religious knowledge or experience that such procedures would not occur to them. Some because of earlier experiences might be threatened or offended by them.

3. Carroll Wise refers to two kinds of religious resources: the tangible and the intangible. The first are external, they are specific things one can do or use, such as Scripture, prayer, religious literature. These are used primarily for educative or supportive purposes, they have a high inspirational value. The intangible resources have to do with religious attitudes and feelings of the counselor himself and the quality of the relationship he can maintain. We deal with this elsewhere. In this discussion we are referring to the tangible resources.

4. The two most familiar religious resources are prayer and Scripture. This is not the place to discuss the efficacy or reality of prayer. We simply recognize that many have gained a sense of gratitude, forgiveness, assurance, commitment, and faith through prayer. Whatever one's theories of biblical interpretation, the Scriptures contain a vivid description of life's destructive forces and life's sustaining and healing forces. Throughout the biblical record the constructive forces are stronger than the destructive forces, love is stronger than hate, forgiveness overcomes guilt, faith is stronger than doubt.

*Modern Man in Search of a Soul (Harcourt Brace, 1939; 1961), p. 264.
**Identity and the Life Cycle (International Universities Press, 1959), pp. 55-56.

94

We would state parenthetically that all counseling is sacred. Whenever an attempt is made to help another in trouble or in need, this is a religious expression, whether or not religious words are used. Using religious terms does not make the act more religious; their absence does not make it less. There was nothing particularly "religious" about the efforts of the Good Samaritan, but it is used as an illustration of man's responsibility to man.

5. There are occasions when religious ideas need to be discussed or tangible religious resources used. Some of these are when doubt, guilt, meaninglessness are a major problem, or when religious support or reassurance is indicated, or when gratitude or joy needs to be expressed.

6. People respond to religious language, symbols, ideas, and practices in different ways. A Quaker, a Baptist, an Episcopalian, a Roman Catholic, a Pentecostal, or an agnostic would respond quite differently to the use of religious resources. Some would be reassured, where others might be embarrassed or even angry. The counselor must be familiar with the religious background of the counselee and sensitive to his responses. He must remember that simple, sincere faith offends no one.

7. Nothing should ever be said or done that embarrasses or offends a person because of his religious background or affiliation.

8. Whether or not the counselor uses religious resources depends upon the person's background, the needs of the situation, and whether or not the counselor can do so sincerely and feel natural in doing so. Such resources are almost always indicated when requested of a pastor.

9. The use or reference to Scripture should be specific and related to a person's needs. The general admonition to "read the Bible" seldom has much value and may create further problems. David Hulme assigns passages for counselees to read supplementary to the sessions which he calls "homework," and he reports some meaningful results. All such procedures necessitate the counselor's having a thoroughgoing, intelligent, pastoral knowledge of Scripture.

10. Many people feel the need of some sort of reality in their religious life. They may request assistance about prayer. They may ask how to pray. Books about the devotional life may have value but should be carefully selected. Books of prayers can be helpful. The devotional classics are valuable with certain groups of people. Prayer with a person can be reassuring, and can serve as a guide that helps him to pray.

11. When prayers or Scriptures are used, they should be brief and usually toward the close of a session. To use them earlier often cuts off discussion.

12. Religious resources can be a strong force and, like any other powerful force, can be misused. When the use of religion embarrasses, increases superstition, or is used to defend false beliefs or hostile actions, it can result in more harm than good. When either prayer, Scripture, or other religious symbols are seen in a pathological context, without protective guidance, the result may be destructive rather than healing.

13. Religious argument is seldom therapeutic and is usually inappropriate in a counseling interview. Rufus Jones says, "Few men are convinced by religious

argument." Besides being ineffective it tends to keep the discussion on an intellectual level, and it can be a means of evading the issue. There are occasions when it is imperative to confront persons with the necessity of evaluating their religious beliefs.

14. A pastor can work with people of other denominations; or with different beliefs than his own. It does not mean he needs to compromise his own convictions; on the contrary he should hold to them. Neither does it mean he imposes them on others.

15. A person's responses to religious ideas and resources are another means of assessing his personality needs. Rigid ideas, authoritarian, dogmatic positions often mean a person is insecure and uncertain. The need to argue, the attempt to force one's ideas on others is motivated by fear. A group in Chicago reports an experiment in which such questions were asked as: What is your earliest memory of a religious experience? What is your favorite Bible story, verse, or character and why? What does prayer mean to you? What do you pray about? What is the most religious act one can perform? What do you consider the greatest sin one could commit? If God could grant you any three wishes, what would they be? The responses were very revealing in terms of persons' personality needs and problems. The article "On the Diagnostic Value of Religious Ideation," by Draper, Meyer, Parzen, and Samuelson, in the Archives of General Psychiatry, September, 1965, pp. 202-7 gives the full list of questions and a description of the study.

16. Seward Hiltner says that one of the unique aspects of pastoral counseling is that the pastor is concerned for the overall healing, salvation, and welfare of the persons.*

FOR FURTHER STUDY: Read widely in the field of prayer, worship, biblical studies, and the psychology of religion. Read in religious biography, noting the resources that proved helpful to the men you read about.

FOR PERSONAL GROWTH: Develop a planned study and meditation program based on devotional literature and the Scriptures for your own personal understanding. Make a serious study of the contents of the prayers of the saints.

RELATING THEORY TO PRACTICE: Books such as Cabot and Dicks's Art of Ministering to the Sick, Oates's Bible in Pastoral Care, and Hulme's Theology and Counseling include lists of Scripture passages that have been useful in pastoral counseling and pastoral care. One can consult these lists and make use of those references that seem most appropriate for his own use. Better yet, make a concentrated study of the Scriptures, compiling your own list of passages that could be used to meet different situations.

*Seward Hiltner and Lowell G. Colston, The Context of Pastoral Counseling (Abingdon Press, 1961), p. 40.

40. UTILIZING THE PUBLIC WORSHIP SERVICE

People who seek pastoral counseling have had various experiences with worship, ranging from those who have found it a deep and moving experience to those who have found it meaningless and irrelevant.

Harry Emerson Fosdick, in a sermon entitled "Why Worship?" makes the following points:

"In worship we are reminded of values that the world makes us forget. . . .

In worship one is carried far enough away from the close-ups of daily life so that one can see the horizons around his living and thus, reorienting himself, regain his sense of direction. . . .

Worship is an experience that rebukes the evil in one's life. . . .

Worship is an experience that rededicates life and so releases its power.*

We would not confuse worship with therapy in either its nature or its purpose; yet common elements of worship, such as confession, adoration, thanksgiving, meditation, and commitment, can be very therapeutic. Many people are helped when public worship is suggested as an adjunct or parallel to counseling.

The following guidelines should be kept in mind:

1. The individual, or family is urged to participate in a church which is meaningful in the light of their present needs and experience.

2. The psychology of individual differences applies in worship as it does everywhere else. Some may find the ritual of a high church Episcopal service very helpful; others may feel that the simplicity of a Quaker meeting "speaks to their condition."

3. Little is accomplished by arguing about worship or insisting that people attend church. This only creates resistance. Interpretation, guidance, or suggestion can be helpful.

4. People need guidance as to the nature and purpose of worship. Many do not find value in worship because they do not understand what the nature of worship is or why the various elements are included. Explanation of such things as the use of symbolism, prayers and scripture, the meaning of the sacraments, and the place of the sermon can make the service more intelligible and purposeful. Helpful literature can also be made available.

5. People should be helped to participate in worship. They should be helped to see that one does not attend worship as he attends other meetings. One does not attend worship as a spectator but as a participant. If a person can be helped to share in worship, he may find it has values that will extend far beyond the counseling session.

*Successful Christian Living (Harper & Bros., 1937), pp. 168-73.

6. People should be helped to realize that meaningful worship does not depend entirely on a good sermon, excellent music, or a beautiful sanctuary. These are helpful but the ultimate value received from worship depends on the attitudes of the worshipers, not the eloquence of the preacher.

7. People should be helped to realize that experiences of worship vary. There are occasions when worship is very meaningful, other occasions when it is not. People should also be helped to realize that the benefits of worship are usually realized over a period of time. One service of worship may produce few if any results, but the accumulative value of many services can produce significant changes in attitudes and feelings.

8. People need to be helped to develop private worship as well as to participate in public worship. It is often (though not always) true that those who benefit most from communal worship also have some expression of private worship. (See Section 41.)

FOR FURTHER STUDY: Study the contents of Fosdick's Pastoral Prayers.

RELATING THEORY TO PRACTICE: In preparation for worship keep specific persons in mind, not to deal with their problems specifically, but to add relevance to the service.

41. THE USE OF PERSONAL RELIGIOUS WORSHIP AS AN ADJUNCT TO COUNSELING SESSIONS

Some persons may ask a pastor directly for help in attaining a more realistic personal religious experience. Others may indicate that such an experience, if it could be developed, would be a source of support and strength.

The best source of information we have of personal worship experiences comes from those sensitive and devoted persons who through the generations have explored the possibilities of the religious life and tested them through long periods of time. Certain common principles from their experiences can be applied to a pastor's counselees.

The traditional expressions of personal religious worship consist of prayer, scripture, inspirational and devotional reading, periods of quiet and meditation. Some utilize one more than another. There are usually elements of all of them present.

1. The religious experiences of the saints grew out of their deep personal sense of need. Because of their realization of their own limitations and inadequacies, they turned to something beyond themselves. They did not start with certainity. They started with a sense of need. They had many doubts, and many questions, but they felt a need for strength, a need for faith, a need for guidance.

2. They did not all secure immediate results. Some did, but many waited for years to find the true values of their efforts. Brother Lawrence, author of the devotional classic The Practice of the Presence of God, had ten years of what he called periods of "dryness," when nothing seemed to happen, before he would speak of the reality as he described it in his book. Anyone who attempts private worship procedures should be reminded that the saints experienced periods of "dryness."

3. The saints all scheduled periods of time for devotional purposes and held to them rather carefully. Some were more consistent in this than others, but unless some specific time is preserved for such activity, it can soon be neglected. The preferred time varies greatly. Some, like Luther, prefer early in the morning; some late in the evening, like John R. Mott. Kagawa got up at three or four in the morning for a period of prayer and then went back to bed. Some saints reserved time daily, some weekly, but most did so regularly. The length of time is not important; some set aside a few minutes, some an hour, a few a whole evening. For most people in our culture a few minutes is more likely to be observed.

4. Bodily postures can be helpful in creating moods, but again there is no uniform practice. Some prefer to kneel, some to sit in a chair, some to stand. Muriel Lester prefers to have her periods of meditation and prayer while walking down the street, while Allen Knight Chalmers found the time spent riding the subway in New York a period which he could utilize for devotional meditation. The presence of many people about him made him aware of his kinship with all mankind.

5. The place for personal worship also can be significant. Many find a sanctuary most helpful, others find a view of nature quiets and expands their thinking. It is usually helpful if a place can be used regularly, but that is not essential.

6. Reading about what others have done can be very suggestive. There are devotional classics that have been helpful for generation after generation. There are devotional guides prepared for this purpose (see the list at the end of this section). Most are inexpensive.

7. The most significant thing to be learned from those who have pioneered in the realm of the spirit, like Brother Lawrence, Thomas a Kempis, John Law, or, more recently, Evelyn Underhill, Rufus Jones, or Harry Emerson Fosdick, is that they demonstrated profound and almost unbelievable results. If we can help persons appropriate something of their experience, it may be as valuable to them as anything else we can do.

The following guidelines should be followed when utilizing personal worship in conjunction with counseling:

Be alert to any clue in the conversation that would indicate a need in the area of personal worship. People may be hesitant in requesting help about such matters.

Allow opportunities for people to raise questions. On occasion clarification of religious ideas is necessary. At times it may seem necessary to confront a person with his unintegrated religious thoughts and to encourage religious self-examination and validation. Religious arguments should be avoided.

Provide the information or guidance necessary for the counselees. Also make them aware of the printed resources that are available. People will often use them, but few people know about them, or where they can be secured.

Be reassuring about the possibilities but do not promise quick and easy solutions. Results can and do take place, but usually after long and continuous effort.

Be sincere. One does not have to have all the answers or have explored all the possibilities himself. We can draw on the experience and testimonies of many. If one has a genuine conviction that reality is there he can impart it to others.

Make most instruction in such matters in the form of suggestions. Avoid the idea of an assignment that a person must do to please the pastor.

FOR FURTHER STUDY: Read the devotional classics.

RELATING THEORY TO PRACTICE: Evaluate any recent or current counseling sessions in the light of the following questions: Could religious worship have been utilized? How could it have been done effectively?

FOR PERSONAL GROWTH: Write out an autobiographical statement of your own devotional or personal religious experience.

PASTORAL AID MATERIALS: Some Classics of the Devotional Life.

> Brother Lawrence, The Practice of the Presence of God
> Thomas a Kempis, The Imitation of Christ
> Walter Rauschenbusch, Prayers of the Social Awakening
> St. Francis of Assisi, The Little Flowers of St. Francis
> Augustine, Confessions
> Friedrich von Hugel, Life of Prayer

More recent writings that have had a wide influence are:

> John Baillie: A Diary of Private Prayer
> Harry Emerson Fosdick: The Meaning of Prayer
> Harry Emerson Fosdick: The Meaning of Faith
> Harry Emerson Fosdick: The Meaning of Service
> Rufus Jones: The Inner World
> George Buttrick: Prayer

There are many more books that can be added to this list. These are listed because they have been so widely used.

42. GUILT, CONFESSION, AND FORGIVENESS

Many people who go to a pastor for help do so because they are suffering from guilt. Biblically speaking they all should be. "All men have sinned and fallen short of the glory of God" (Romans 3:23). The problem of guilt has deep theological and psychological implications that every pastor must be prepared to face.

The Bible is filled with allusions to sin, guilt, confession, and forgiveness.

> "Have mercy on me, O God,
> according to thy steadfast love;
> according to thy abundant mercy
> blot out my transgressions...
>
> For I know my transgressions,
> and my sin is ever before me."--Psalm 51:1-3

> "When I declared not my sin,
> my body wasted away."--Psalm 32:1

> "If we confess our sins, he is faithful and just,
> and will forgive our sins and cleanse us from all
> unrighteousness."--I John 1:9

Historically, theologians from Augustine to Paul Tillich have grappled with the problem of guilt. The church has used many methods for dealing with guilt. In the early church, confession was public and informal. In the Catholic Church it became private, mandatory, and sacramental. In the Anglican Church it was modified and not mandatory. The Reformers objected to its abuses but advocated that confession be made to the minister, but after first being made to God. The revival movement utilized the mourner's bench. In one way or another the church has attempted to help man resolve his guilt, although in Protestantism there is no universal procedure.

People who go to a pastor for help represent very different religious backgrounds. This is especially true at an ecumenical counseling center but is also true even within a local church. People will have quite different experiences and expectations regarding guilt, confession, and forgiveness, depending on whether their backgrounds have been Catholic, Episcopalian, Unitarian, Southern Baptist, Christian Scientist, Pentecostal, agnostic, or humanistic.

Ever since the days of Freud (and even before) psychologists have been studying the phenomenon of guilt. Psychotherapists of all schools deal with guilt in their clients and patients, but they also vary greatly in their treatment of guilt.

Guilt is both a theological and psychological problem. According to Edward V. Stein, in his book <u>Guilt: Theory and Therapy</u>, "guilt is experienced as conflict, tension, anxiety, depression, remorse."* These are terms that deal with deep psy-

*(Westminster Press, 1968), p. 31.

chological matters. One cannot deal with guilt without considering values, morals, sin, repentance, forgiveness, and the nature of God. These are profound theological issues.

The pastor must be able to distinguish between real guilt and neurotic guilt, between guilt that is deserved or partially deserved, guilt related to actual wrong, and guilt that is undeserved or partially undeserved, guilt that may be related to faulty training or unfortunate circumstances. The pastor must recognize the needs of the person who discusses guilt too lightly and the one who cannot accept forgiveness.

People try in many ways to endure or alleviate the burden of guilt. Some try to suppress it, or worse to repress it, to bury it, to deny it exists. Some try to rationalize it, to explain it away, to justify it. Some try to project it on to others. Some try to forget it in an endless round of activities, in a mad search for pleasure, in doing good works, in a self-imposed penance. Some try to expiate it. Some try to endure it, to stoically "live with it"--neither of which works.

The religious or traditional confessional approach to guilt is repentance, penitence, confession, restitution, absolution, the acceptance of God's forgiveness, newness of life. It is based upon the central faith in the grace of God, the faith one has that God is a God of love, God forgives, God redeems, and God restores.

When dealing with neurotic guilt, the pastor would find the method indicated to be counseling. When the guilt is morbid, extreme, or accompanied by other pathologies, the patient should be referred for psychiatric treatment or evaluation. To treat neurotic guilt by confessional methods without an awareness of the psychological involvements could increase the patient's morbid sense of guilt. Properly applied confessional methods used by a pastor can be effective in relieving all forms of guilt. When a person has real or normal guilt, it would indicate that, in conjunction with counseling, the confessional methods could be used. Since most persons experience both real and neurotic guilt, they need both counseling and a confessional approach.

When a person manifests a complete absence of any guilt, it indicates the possible presence of psychopathic tendencies or complete hopelessness. The counselor should move slowly and with great caution. A psychopath (or sociopath) does not respond to counseling and should be referred.

Hearing a confession of guilt is a sacred responsibility. Wayne Oates sees the confession not merely as something the person is confessing to the minister but as something he is confessing to God, so he receives it "as unto God and not unto himself. He was privileged to listen as the person told this to God, not to him."*

The confessional approach to guilt and forgiveness lends itself to a use of religious resources. At times, a brief prayer, a verse of scripture, if such are natural, are more meaningful than anything else. (See Section 39, Religious Resources.)

*Protestant Pastoral Counseling, pp. 176-77.

The hearing of confessions raises the whole question of ethics of communication. Some things that are revealed under such conditions should not be included in records. (See Section 31.)

FOR FURTHER STUDY: Read one or more of the studies that relate psychological findings to theological thought, such as David Belgum's Guilt: Where Religion and Psychology Meet; Edward Stein's Guilt, Theory and Therapy; or James Knight's Conscience and Guilt. Also it would be informative to read material on the Catholic Confessional to understand how one branch of Christendom has handled this problem.

FOR PERSONAL GROWTH: Write out in your own words your understanding of the meaning of grace and forgiveness.

RELATING THEORY TO PRACTICE: Evaluate any counseling experiences for evidences of guilt. Consider whether the guilt expressed would be neurotic guilt or real guilt. Consider also whether the approach indicated is the confessional approach or the counseling approach.

PASTORAL AID MATERIALS: Wayne Oates suggests several passages of Scripture that could be helpful in working with people troubled by guilt.*

Isaiah 1:18	Romans 8:26
Matthew 11:28-30	I John 3:19,20
I John 1:9	John 8:11, 31
Hebrews 4:15-16	I John 3:1-3

Check the references in the Scripture on guilt, grace, and forgiveness and develop a list of your own.

_____   _____
_____   _____
_____   _____

43. CONVERSION

Counseling and evangelism have much in common but are basically two different functions. In counseling one does not usually attempt to convert another to his point of view. Some people who seek pastoral counseling may want to discuss

*The Bible in Pastoral Care (Westminster Press, 1963), p. 97.

their religious experiences; others as a result of counseling may have a conversion experience. Certain factors should be kept in mind.

Conversion is a psychological as well as a spiritual phenomenon. William James gave the classical definition in his famous book The Varieties of Religious Experience when he said, "to be converted, to be regenerated, to receive grace, to experience religion, to gain an assurance are so many phrases which denote the process gradual or sudden, by which a self hitherto divided and consciously wrong, inferior and unhappy, becomes unified and consciously right, superior and happy, in consequnce of its firmer hold upon religious realities." As a psychologist James did not attempt to define what these realities were, but he did not doubt either their presence or their influence.

Conversion does not necessarily need to be religious. Men can be converted to communism, to democracy, or even to a point of view.

People experience conversion in different ways. This was true both biblically and historically. Jeremiah's experience was different from Isaiah's, Peter's was different from Paul's, Augustine had a different experience from that of John Wesley, George Fox's was different from Horace Bushnell's, yet all were converted.

There are denominational differences in what is expected in the conversion experience. The evangelical churches have different expectations from the liturgical churches. There are also differences within the membership of one congregation.

Conversion can be gradual or sudden, as William James recognized in the definition above. It may be dramatic, cataclysmic (although even in these cases we feel there was a longer period of preparation), or it may be gradual, happen over a long period of time.

There are certain common elements or patterns that are present in most conversion experiences.

a. There is a period of preparation, often called a period of "unrest." Starbuck, in his pioneer study on the psychology of conversion, said the actual conversion experience was usually preceded by "a mental state known as 'conviction' or the 'sense of sin'." Some of the words he uses to describe this state are very similar to those sometimes used to describe the state of mind in which people seek counseling. They include "feelings of imperfection, incompleteness, unworthiness, a sense of estrangement from God, doubts and questionings, depression and sadness, restlessness, anxiety and uncertainty, and the various bodily affections."*

b. There is also an awareness of better possibilities. At times this may be a very uncertain feeling, only a wishful hope, but there has to be an awareness of new possibilites. One has to be converted to something. Both elements must be present: (1) the dissatisfaction with things as they are, and (2) the new possibility.

c. Both a and b result in the act of commitment. This is the change of direction required by the New Testament in the word "repent." It is an act of faith and trust. According to Alan Richardson, in his Theological Word Book of the Bible, repentance means turning from sin and turning to God. As he puts it, "Re-

*Starbuck, Psychology of Religion, p. 58.

104

pentance thus means much more than being sorry for one's misdeeds; it involves an active acceptance of God's gift of faith."*

d. As a result of c one gains a new sense of identity within faith. As Wayne Oates puts it, "The conversion experience for many is the beginning of their true selfhood."** This results in a sense of inner peace, integrity, and purpose. It gives one a new awareness of being "accepted by God." Hopefully this will also result in a new sense of dedication and commitment to the common good and mark the beginning of continued growth.

People experience conversion at different levels and to different degrees.

There are pseudo conversions that are the result of momentary feelings, the pressure of the crowd, the persuasiveness of a speaker. There is no permanence to them.

There is a superficial conversion that may be sincere in one respect but does not take into account the fact that a new orientation in life and new patterns of conduct are difficult to maintain, and the initial experience soon loses its influence.

There is the partial conversion, which may be confined to certain areas of living and be very incomplete. One great religious spirit said, "I have had to be converted many times. I had to be converted about Christ. I had to be converted about race. I had to be converted about money, etc."

There is the conversion experience that actually is symptomatic of an emotional disturbance, even of a psychotic break. The pastor must be very careful in assessing such behavior.

There is the conversion that is genuine, profound, and changes one's being. This may be a sudden experience, dramatic and conclusive. Or the experience may be gradual, over a period of time, with no single event that can be pinpointed in time or space.

There are those persons and groups that hold that conversion, by it's very nature, involves a sudden, dramatic and permanent change in life-styles. There are others who feel that religion requires repeated peak experiences which are understood as a part of one's total religious experience.

One test of the validity of a conversion experience is time. If the new quality of life, the sense of inner security and peace continues, the reality of the experience is indicated. Many conversions which are superficial, the result of the influence of the crowd or the persuasiveness of an evangelist do not survive the test of time.

Another test is the quality of life which follows the conversion. The Christian virtues of humility, sincerity, courage, and compassion are increased and perpetuated when the conversion is real. When such virtues are lacking, doubt is cast on the reality of the conversion.

*(The Macmillan Co., 1950), p. 192.
**The Christian Pastor (Westminster Press, 1951), p. 15.

There is usually a human agent in most conversions. William Booth, founder of the Salvation Army, said, "The first vital step in saving outcasts consists in making them feel that some decent human being cares enough for them to take an interest in the question whether they rise or sink."*

FOR FURTHER STUDY: Read in the field of the psychology of religion, particularly William James's <u>Varieties of Religious Experience</u>.

FOR PERSONAL GROWTH: Study all passages dealing with conversion in the New Testament. Write out an autobiographical statement of your own conversion experience.

44. ADJUNCTS TO COUNSELING

In addition to the specific concerns that are discussed during the counseling hour the pastor may recognize that the person's pattern of living contributes to an overall sense of frustration, fatigue, or pressure. The development of some skills or the alteration of some habits may do much to alleviate the tension or add to the interest and purpose in a person's life. The pastor may suggest tasks, a change of patterns, the following of certain procedures that the person can do outside of counseling. They may be as important as what takes place within the interview.

Some of the most common procedures that can be recommended are rest, recreation, and the cultivation of a hobby. These are very similar to the kinds of things a doctor recommends when he suggests a patient get more rest, get out-of-doors, or take a vacation.

Some suggestions, such as reading (see Section 45, "Bibliotherapy") or attending classes in church or community, may be made to provide more information in certain areas, so people can make more intelligent decisions, or expand their interests.

Service projects can be very useful. Some people need to forget their own concerns in the interest of others or a cause as much as they need therapy.

1. When using such adjuncts to counseling it should be remembered that each person is unique; what appeals to one may not appeal to another. All such suggestions should take into account the individual's interests, aptitude, available time, etc.

2. It must also be recognized that there are times when suggestions for supplementary activities are more important than others. Exercise, reading, etc.,

*Begbie, <u>Twice Born Men</u>, p. 22.

106

should only be suggested when a person's physical and emotional state is such that he can profit from it.

3. Such suggestions should not be made in such a way that they add to the person's pressures. If a person feels he has failed the counselor, or sees the assignment as something that must be fulfilled, the assignment may add to his frustration.

4. Activities outside counseling should not be conceived as substitutes for the counseling process. They are adjuncts that supplement but do not replace counseling.

5. It is preferable if the counselee can help in the selecting of supplementary activities. It requires much ingenuity to find things for some people to do because of limits of time, interest, etc., but the results are worth it.

FOR FURTHER STUDY: Read in the field of recreational therapy.

FOR PERSONAL GROWTH: Write out your philosophy of play, rest and relaxation.

45. BIBLIOTHERAPY

One of the major supplementary resources of counseling is the printed page. The wisdom of the world is found in books. Men have condensed lifetimes of study and experience between the covers of books and made them available to anyone who will read.

Technically this is known as bibliotherapy. Bibliotherapy is defined as "the prescription of reading materials which will help develop emotional maturity and nourish and sustain the development of intellectual maturity, which is an essential component of the total personality."

The pastor should have available a small loan library for use in his counseling. This can be provided by the church or a counseling center. It is much more effective to have a book at hand and make it available at once than to send a person to the library, although this can also be suggested when necessary.

Certain principles or guidelines should be observed in the use of reading materials.

1. Reading is no substitute for counseling. It can be an excellent supplement that will add depth to the counseling process, and it can frequently be used parallel to counseling.

2. Reading is for several purposes: recreation, information, education, inspiration. All can be useful supplementary aids to counseling. Some persons need relaxing, enjoyable reading; some need information in order to make decisions or understand situations; others need the reassurance, courage, and hope that comes from devotional or inspirational reading.

3. Information is available, prepared by authorities in many areas of concern that frequently confront the pastor, such as marriage and family, sex, alcoholism, vocational guidance, mental illness, mental retardation, study habits, religious doubt, prayer, faith, etc.

4. People as a whole are not familiar with the literature that is available on various topics. It is the pastor's (counselor's) responsibility to acquaint them with it.

5. Reading can save much time in the interview. There is no need to spend time telling a person something that he can read just as well--or better. Interview time can be spent discussing the person's feelings and questions about what he has read.

6. Reading lends authority. (Sometimes it lends too much--there is a common illusion that because something is in print it is true.) The pastor cannot be an authority in all fields, but he can make use of the experience of the specialists who have put their experience in print. An authority may reinforce the pastor's position.

7. Short reading assignments are usually better than long ones. Some of the best information is in pamphlet form. A pamphlet has several advantages: It is concise, it can be read at one sitting, and it is inexpensive.

8. Reading is most valuable when the material is discussed with the counselor after it has been read. It helps the counselee to clarify his thinking, resolve questions, and reinforce his learning. It also provides the counselor insights into the person's needs. People react to books in different ways.

9. There is a great variation in the value of printed materials. Some information is very limited, some is faulty, some is out-of-date. Some self-help literature is extremely sentimental, moralistic, and superficial. For a counselor to suggest inadequate material will limit the counseling process and destroy the counselee's confidence in the counselor.

10. A counselor should only suggest reading with which he is personally familiar. There may be exceptions to this, such as material recommended by an authority, but, in the main, it is a good principle. To suggest something without checking its accuracy and reliability borders on the unethical.

11. Reading should be suggested in terms of the individual. Age, education, temperament, emotional condition, and the time available for reading all influence the reading one should suggest, and whether one should suggest reading at all.

12. The counselor should be familiar with a variety of material. Material that appeals to one may be uninteresting to another.

13. Some do not respond well to reading assignments or suggestions. For some, reading is almost a foreign experience. The average person reads only one or two books a year. (Clergymen average ten or twelve.) Many people have never read a serious book. The higher the intellectual and educational level of the counselee, the more effective bibliotherapy is likely to be.

14. When a person requests a book on a subject--family life, for example, it may be that he wants to talk about that problem. However, the book should be provided. An opportunity to discuss the problem should also be made possible.

15. At times a pastor (counselor) may need to discourage reading. Some people overidentify and erroneously interpret what they read. This is especially true of persons under stress. The powers of suggestion are very great. At times it is well for some persons to refrain from reading.

16. Reading should not be advocated in such a way that it adds to the person's problems. It should usually be mentioned as a suggestion, as an elective that is available. The person should not be put in the position of feeling guilty if he doesn't fulfill the counselor's assignments.

17. Sometimes the concepts and content of a book can be better abosrbed if the counselee is encouraged to actually purchase the book itself.

FOR PERSONAL GROWTH: Plan a three-month program of reading for personal growth and enrichment. Keep a record of your progress and experiences.

46. FREE WRITING

John Woolman, John Wesley, John R. Mott, and many other men of great spiritual depth and power had one thing in common. They all kept a journal or a dairy or a notebook wherein they recorded their deepest thoughts and concerns. How much this practice contributed to their insight, to their self-understanding, and to the attainment of their goals we do not know--our opinion would be that it had great practical value. Undoubtedly, Augustine received significant personal help from writing his "confessions," as Pascal did in writing his "thoughts."

Many people when confronted with a decision have found that listing the pros and cons on a piece of paper helps them weigh the alternatives. Some have found it an aid to their devotional life if they write out their prayers.

Counselors have found it a good supplement to counseling sessions to have a counselee write out his feelings.

Fred McKinney in his book Counseling for Personal Adjustment advises persons who are troubled with a problem, or who are seeking growth in character and personality, to do what he calls "free writing." This consists simply of expressing on paper one's thoughts or feelings. He says this practice is quite effective in time of tension. He advises persons to write in any way they wish and as rapidly as they can until the tension is reduced and some understanding is achieved. He says:

"The important aspect of this project is that it is completely free. Allow every idea and feeling that comes to you to arise, and write at least something down. No one has to read it, not even you. You don't have to put into action what you write down. In fact, often after you express a feeling it is no longer strong. You may feel different after writing it. If the end result of this free expression is relaxation and a few clear ideas about yourself and your plans, then it has been effective."*

Phillips and Wiener, in their book Short-Term Therapy, include a discussion of what they call "writing therapy." They describe how it has been used in a college counseling clinic to meet the pressures of a waiting list. When a counselor does not have time to see all the clients seeking help, he has some write out their problems and let him evaluate and comment on them. While no adequate research on this practice exists as yet, there have been very favorable results.

There seems to be little question that for some, personal growth, new insights, and deeper understanding can come as a result of such procedures.

When it is necessary for a counselee to miss a week, either because he cannot come, or the pastor cannot meet him, it is sometimes helpful for the person to take the same time and write out his feelings. If a counselee finds it difficult to express himself in the counseling sessions, it may help him to write out his feelings. Sometimes it enables a counselee to progress faster if he spends some time between sessions doing "free writing."

Instructions for the free-writing procedure should include some guidelines to be followed. The counselor should suggest to the counselee that:

--they set a time and place for the writing, but do not make it an assignment so the counselee feels guilty if he does not complete it.

--they ignore penmanship, grammar, and punctuation. It should be an experience of free expression, not authorship.

--they be frank, honest, and specific.

--they destroy, or place where it will not be seen by others, any embarrassing or personal material.

--the free writing be brought to the next counseling session or mailed in prior to the appointment.

--they include concerns and problems but also goals and aspirations; that they be positive; that they never complete a statement without listing some of the strengths (this is important).

The same procedure may be followed, and the same value obtained, by encouraging the counselee to paint, draw, or model instead of write.

FOR PERSONAL GROWTH: At least once a week, over a two- or three-month period, experiment with free writing yourself.

RELATING THEORY TO PRACTICE: Suggest to some of your counselees that they do some free writing as a supplement to counseling. Whenever an appointment must be canceled, have the counselee use the time to do some free writing.

*McKinney, Counseling for Personal Adjustment, p. 45.

47. COUNSELING THE POOR AND DISADVANTAGED

Poverty is one of the major social problems of our generation. On occasion a pastor will be called upon to work with someone from a poverty area. Some pastors are serving churches in marginal communities or in a poverty area. A poverty area is a community characterized by poor housing, low wages, and unemployment, limited and inadequate medical services, educational dropouts, racial prejudice and suspicion, and other problems associated with the lower socio-economic communities.

Those who work in these areas should keep certain factors in mind.

1. The culture of poverty destroys aspiration, results in resignation, and eliminates hope. On the other hand, some find it protective and are fearful of being overwhelmed by more demanding cultural milieus. Michael Harrington, in his book The Other America, a report on "Poverty in the United States," says, "Poverty in the United States is a culture, an institution, a way of life." He goes on to say that this culture of poverty "is becoming increasingly populated by those who do not belong to anybody or anything. . . . Their horizon has become more and more restricted: they see one another, and that means they see little reason for hope."*

2. People in poverty areas usually have multiple problems--housing, family, jobs, limited education--all of which create a vicious cycle of more problems, no success, loss of aspiration, and loss of hope.

3. Most pastoral care literature has been patterned after a type of counseling that has proved effective with middle- and upper-class members of society. The same method has not always been found effective in working with the poor. Poor people are unfamiliar with counseling by appointment, they find difficulty in verbalization, and they do not see how talking about a problem can help. They think in terms of action, information, or advice. They are more action-oriented than conversation-oriented.

4. The primary concerns of the poor are immediate, concrete, and practical. They need funds, a job, vocational training, food, housing, etc.

5. To work with the disadvantaged one must know the social welfare resources that are available. (See Section 27, "Psychiatric Referral.") The disadvantaged are not aware of them, they are often suspicious of them, or they feel there is no use in trying to get help.

6. The education level of the poor is often low, their schooling has been limited and often substandard. Many are illiterate. They have a language all their own which is called "street talk" or "ghettoese." Their vocabulary of basic English is limited. Communication with them may be difficult or even nonexistent unless the counselor is careful of the words he uses.

7. The poor look with suspicion on others not in their culture. The law, the upper class, and the church are figures and institutions they have not often known, and when they have, have often been mistreated or patronized by them. A counselor's first and most basis task is to respect and understand the problems faced by these people and by so doing secure their trust.

*(Macmillan, 1962), pp. 22, 18.

8. The experience of the disadvantaged with religion has been very limited. There are exceptions but for the majority this is true. Many have no religious affiliation at all. Most have not known a pastoral relationship as the average Protestant church conceives it. Some have been attracted to "storefront" churches, emotional sects. They are not without religious feelings, hopes, and aspirations. Religion as it is known in suburbia or taught in seminary is very foreign to them.

9. These persons are "children of God." They have needs, hopes, feelings. No one really knows the answers to the immense problems of the ghetto, the racial strife, the loneliness, frustration, bitterness, and despair that characterize the poor in America. No one has had overwhelming success working with individuals and their problems, let alone solving the great social dilemmas. They do respond to understanding, support, guidance--but it takes great patience, perseverance, and faith to reach them.

FOR FURTHER GROWTH: Read all references to the poor or disadvantaged in the Encyclopedia of Social Work. Read any recent studies on poverty.

RELATING THEORY TO PRACTICE: Evaluate all counseling with the disadvantaged asking specific questions. How much do material matters influence their situation? How much does the culture of poverty shape their behavior? Do the methods advocated by most books in pastoral care apply here?

COMMUNITY RESOURCES:

	Name	Phone	Address
Welfare Office	_____	_____	_____
Salvation Army	_____	_____	_____
Volunteers of America	_____	_____	_____
Employment Service	_____	_____	_____
Office of Economic Opportunity	_____	_____	_____

48. MATERIAL AID AND PRACTICAL ASSISTANCE

Some people go to a pastor to express a need for financial help, housing, employment, food, etc. This is particularly true with those in the poverty area, and also with the elderly, the transient, etc. This fact raises definite questions and some perplexing problems. No one wants to see another person going hungry, but neither do we want to subsidize vagrancy. It raises further the whole question of the pastor's role, his relationship with other professionals and other agencies.

The Bible is filled with admonitions to feed the hungry, clothe the naked, care for the homeless, minister to the poor and unfortunate. No real studies have been made as to how the pastor should and can do this most effectively in the twentieth century.

Certain principles should guide us.

1. It is recognized that for some persons, particularly in the poverty area, physical needs are paramount. It does little good to attempt counseling a person who is hungry, worried because he is out of a job, or in need of housing. Once the physical needs have been met, the pastor can move on to other concerns.

2. The psychological effects of unemployment, inadequate housing, inadequate medical care, etc., are more severe and far-reaching than the physical effects.

3. Recognizing and helping with the physical needs of a person can be a pastor's means of establishing a relationship that can lead to opportunities to help with other problems. When one does help with such matters, he should do so in such a way that the person really helps himself and does not lose his sense of integrity or respect.

4. It is generally considered unwise to lend money or give gifts to one with whom one is counseling. It can be detrimental to the relationship.

5. In order to understand the problems and feelings of those who are hungry, out of work, or without adequate housing, one must make a definite effort to see things from the counselee's perspective and position, rather than from any preconceived bias or concepts of the pastor. This is not easy to do, but can be done.

6. There are persons who are professional panhandlers. They go to all the agencies, and they are skilled at eliciting sympathy and securing loans or gifts. They usually find the clergy quite easy to deceive.

7. There are agencies, both public and private, that do offer assistance of many kinds. The pastor should know and work with such groups as the county and state welfare, old age assistance, the Salvation Army, Travelers Aid, etc. They have training, skill, experience, and resources he seldom has.

8. It is possible the person may be fragmented by dealing with many agencies, or be discouraged and depersonalized by the treatment he receives from some persons. The pastor maintains a personal relationship through all his experiences and enables him to maintain his integrity and respect at all times.

COMMUNITY RESOURCES: List the places where material aid might be provided.
Welfare Department _____

Salvation Army _____

Veterans Administration _____

Travelers Aid _____

49. PASTORAL CARE OF SHUT-INS

Among the most neglected persons in America are the shut-ins and the homebound. Every pastor should have the shut-ins or homebound high on his list of priorities. Otherwise they will be pushed into the background and receive the leftovers of his time and effort.

Certain principles should be kept in mind.

The homebound represent all ages, ranging from the spastic child to the elderly person; however, the majority are older persons. They represent all levels of economic life. Some have no financial concerns, others are depending on welfare for mere subsistence.

They are located in many places. Some live with their families, some in single rooms, some in nursing homes. Housing is one of their chief concerns.

They represent a wide variety of personality patterns and emotional responses. Some are creative, courageous, cheerful, and inspiring. Some are struggling to maintain their courage, living lives of quiet resignation. Some have lost their creativity and have become bitter and resentful. All need help.

Some common concerns expressed by shut-ins are health, financial worries, forced inactivity, loneliness, boredom, housing, neglect by family, uncertainty about the future, fear of being a burden to others, religious doubt, etc. Each person is unique, each one has his own problems and concerns--the one thing common to all is the physical and emotional condition which creates their situation.

Their sources of strength are the capacity to maintain interest in things, reading, hobbies, current events--anything; a sense of humor, a concern for others, a philosophy of life (which usually goes back many years), good relationships with friends and family, pleasant surroundings, courage, and a profound religious faith.

The Pastoral Call

Just to remember the shut-in is one thing. If one calls on a shut-in--does nothing more than break the monotony of continuous days that are all the same--he has rendered a service.

1. A call is for the purpose of establishing friendship, expressing concern and interest. For the pastor this is natural.

2. The pastor calls as a representative of the church. He symbolizes the fellowship of the local congregation, the tradition of the Christian faith, and the brotherhood of Christianity.

3. The pastor calls to listen. So few people have the time or the interest to let these homebound people talk, express their concerns, share their points of view. In addition to listening the pastor provides reassurance and support. This is primarily a supportive ministry. The use of religious resources, especially with older persons, can be very meaningful.

4. On occasion a shut-in will raise questions or seek counseling concerning personal or family problems. If so, the problem should be dealt with. This kind of situation causes one to shift from supportive to problem-solving procedures.

5. Some need very practical help, such as assistance in shopping, making a phone call, mailing letters, etc. Such services in themselves can be of real

practical and symbolic value. They show that somebody cares. On occasion some-one may need to notify the person's resident pastor, enlist the help of some lay men or women, or secure the services of a social agency.

6. In ministering to these persons one also is rendering a service to their families. If they can be sustained and helped, then others are also helped as a result.

7. A further value grows out of the fact that in ministering to such persons, the pastor himself receives a benefit.

FOR PERSONAL GROWTH: Study the scriptural passages in reference to the elderly and unfortunate, and write out your philosophy of pastoral care to the shut-in and the elderly.

RELATING THEORY TO PRACTICE: Keep a record of all calls to shut-ins and note areas of conversation, needs expressed, etc.

COMMUNITY RESOURCES:

	Name	Phone	Address
Council on the Aging	_____	_____	_____
Old-Age Assistance Office	_____	_____	_____

50. KEEPING RECORDS

There are several reasons why a pastor should keep complete and accurate records. There is no value in keeping records for records' sake. Records are meant to be used for specific purposes.

1. Records are kept to enable one to render a more significant service to a parishioner/counselee. It is not enough to trust one's memory from week to week. Careful records make possible better counseling.

2. Records are a means whereby one can improve his effectiveness. Only as a pastor studies and evaluates his experience will he be aware of his errors and increase his understanding and counseling skills. The very process of writing down an experience forces one to reflect on what happened.

3. Records are a means of making more effective referrals. When one makes a referral to a psychiatrist or a social agency it is well to have a thorough record to apprise them of the person's problems and what occurred in your relationship.

4. Records are a necessity for adequate supervision if one is in a training program, or for consultation if one is in a parish and needs to consult a specialist about a counselee.

5. Records could be the means of some needed research.

Guidelines for the Keeping of Records

1. Keep a record of every interview.

2. Do not record any information that would be incriminating or unduly embarrassing to the counselee. Someone else might see the records or they might be subpoenaed. This kind of material can be remembered anyway.

3. Record all pertinent matter--but keep the records brief.

4. Record any meaningful or pertinent conversation.

5. Record any nonverbal clues or indications of feelings.

6. Include personal evaluations in parenthesis or at the end of the record. (See the example at the end of this section.)

7. Leave ample space for later evaluation by yourself or a supervisor or consultant.

8. If a session is taped--and this should only be done with the person's permission--notes for the file can be taken from the tape.

9. If notes are taken during a session, it should be with the person's permission. He should be assured that you are putting down ideas for your own use and that no one else will have access to these notes. Often only a key word or phrase is all that needs to be jotted down. This helps maintain accuracy and saves time later. If this is done, one should be careful to maintain frequent eye contact and be sure that the taking of notes is not interfering with the counseling process. Taking notes during an interview can cause the counselor to focus on content rather than the relationship. If any of these undesirable factors occurs, one should cease making notes and concentrate solely on the conversation. Remember also that the taking of notes can reenforce the production of certain material so one should be cautious at this point.

10. Notes can arouse suspicions in a counselee. If the pastor feels this is happening, he may ask him if he would like to see the notes, or assure him that they will be destroyed following the interview.

11. When notes are not taken during an interview, it is wise to jot down things to be remembered immediately after the interview.

12. Study the records of previous contacts with a person prior to an interview, and then study and evaluate what took place after an interview.

RELATING THEORY TO PRACTICE: Everyone should develop a record system that is natural for him. The following is a suggested pattern to follow. List counselee's conversation more or less as it occurs. Put your own comments in rounded parentheses (   ). Put any observations or evaluations in square brackets [   ]. Include here all significant feelings that are expressed, nonverbal clues, etc. Leave a wide margin on one side for later evaluation and notes as illustrated in the example that follows.

Name Doe, John   Date June 19, 19--   Time 3:30 P.M.

"I was so angry at my boss I could hardly speak. I almost lost my voice I was so mad."

(You just couldn't control yourself.)

"Yes. It was like in the army, everyone wants to order you around."

[Clenching and unclenching of fists, tears in eyes.]

"You never get away from it. I've got a boss on the job, a boss at home."

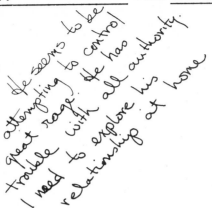

51. THE PROBLEM OF FEES

The question of fees in pastoral counseling is new and still somewhat controversial. The pastor of a church usually does not receive fees from members of his congregation. His parishioners contribute to the church, or should. People who are not members of his church but come to the pastor for counseling should and often do make a contribution to the church as an expression of appreciation for the help they have received. The whole question of fees, payment for services, the need of the person to give, etc., is still a matter that needs to be explored.

When a pastor is working in a pastoral counseling center which is sponsored by a church, council of churches, or a seminary, usually a fee is charged.

Experience testifies to the fact that it is good for the counselee to pay a fee for several reasons. Some of these reasons are:

Allowing a person to contribute enhances his self-esteem.

Allowing a person to contribute decreases his dependency feelings.

Allowing a person to contribute enables him to give as well as receive. This is extremely important.

When a policy of charging fees is established, certain principles and procedures are usually followed.

1. The fee is discussed with the counselee at the initial interview.

2. The fee is fixed on a sliding scale, according to the counselee's income, as is done in most agencies.

3. No financial investigation is made of any individual or family.

4. The individual, in some situations, is permitted to assess his own fee.

5. No one is refused help because of lack of funds.

6. A minimum fee of one dollar may be asked of students or others with limited funds. Some counselors simply provide free service to these.

7. When other services, such as psychological testing, psychiatric evaluation, or medical prescription, are indicated, the fee for this is settled between the counselee and the specialist.

8. A person should feel free to discuss the fee with the counselor, since it may have a bearing on the counseling.

Experience indicates that those who cannot contribute should be given the opportunity to do something definite and specific for the pastor, the church, or for some other community service. This is based on the principle that one should not receive unless he also gives. We become stronger as we help others. Working this out requires much ingenuity. A contribution cannot be demanded, but it is important to keep the principle in mind.

FOR PERSONAL GROWTH: Write out your own philosophy of money. Include your feelings about receiving it in payment for services, and the need of persons to give.

RELATING THEORY TO PRACTICE: List things persons might do in exchange for counseling services, other than contribute fees.

52. TOWARD A CODE OF ETHICS

No strict or formal code of ethics can cover pastoral counseling or pastoral care. It is far too complicated and complex for that. However, there are certain general principles that should govern the pastoral counselor's work.

1. Every individual is seen as a child of God and therefore as a person of unconditional worth.

2. Christian love is the one basic factor that underlies, and at times determines, the methods, techniques, and procedures one follows.

3. The ultimate well-being or the maximum good for the person is the determining factor in the goals and objectives of all pastoral efforts.

In the light of these more or less inclusive principles there are several guides, or rules of conduct that govern the work of a pastor.

Responsibility to the Counselee

The pastor will treat all conversation and all information in the strictest confidence. The only exception: when a person is so disturbed it becomes necessary to notify his family or physician. Even then he should be informed it is being done.

The counselee will always be told the truth. There could be occasions when, for physical or emotional reasons, some information might need to be withheld for a period of time. The principle still stands that each person will be dealt with honestly and truthfully.

The pastor will be responsible in all of his counseling relationships. Just as the physician is expected to be thorough in his treatment of physical ills, so the pastor must be thorough in his treatment of emotional, moral, or spiritual ills.

The pastor will function as a pastoral counselor and not attempt to play the role of doctor, psychiatrist, attorney, social worker, or other specialist.

The pastor will utilize all resources that are available. He will not attempt to perform a function some other professional person can do better.

The pastor shall speak cautiously in any diagnosis or prognosis. He will not make unwarranted promises or create false hope.

The pastor will show no favoritism because of wealth, position, race, denomination, or personality characteristics. All will receive his best efforts.

If a pastor feels he cannot function effectively with a person, he will suggest that he be referred to another pastor or another counselor.

Responsibility to Other Professions

The pastor works cooperatively with other professions and agencies. He refers to pastors, physicians, social workers, attorneys, psychiatrists; he receives referrals from all these people as well. In all relationships with other professions he will act professionally, handle all information confidentially, and render any assistance possible. At no time shall a pastor speak disparagingly of members of other professions to counselees.

Responsibility to Himself

The pastor has a responsibility to himself and his family. For his own well-being and the well-being of the people he serves, he should maintain himself at the peak of efficiency physically, emotionally, and spiritually.

FOR FURTHER STUDY: Read in the field of Christian ethics in general. Read the codes of ethics of the American Medical Association, The American Psychological Association, etc.

FOR PERSONAL GROWTH: Write out in your own words the principles that will guide your own practice of pastoral care.

53. THE NATURE OF MAN

The pastor does all his counseling from a particular stance or point of view. He approaches all persons from the perspective of the Christian faith and the Christian view of man. It is very easy to forget this and slip into the pattern of seeing man from a humanistic, or even a mechanistic, point of view. Psychiatric, psychological, and sociological interpretations can be so interesting, precise, authoritative, and often helpful that it is easy for the pastor to forget that he has a distinct and all-important point of view of his own.

Many volumes have been written on the doctrine of Man. Many different points of view have been expressed. Each person must work out his own convictions for himself. The following are some guidelines that are suggested to stimulate further thought.

1. Man is a child of God, created in his image, the object of his love. This means that every person who goes to a pastor is a child of God. Before he is a counselee or a parishioner he is a child of God. He is not a problem or a case, he is a person. No matter what he has done, no matter how degraded, maladjusted, hostile, or resistant to the pastor's services he may be, he is still a child of God, of infinite worth in his sight, and must be seen as such. "See what love the Father has given us, that we should be called children of God; and so we are." (I John 3:1.)

2. Man is finite and dependent. His knowledge is limited, his capacities are limited, he is dependent on others and on God for his very existence, for meaning in life, and for his ultimate fulfillment.

3. Man is a sinner in need of grace and redemption. This includes the counselor as well as the counselee, the pastor as well as the parishioner. "All have sinned and fall short of the glory of God." (Romans 3:23.) God's grace and forgiveness are available to man. This is the heart of the gospel.

4. Man is in process. He is in a constant state of becoming. He has the capacity to look backward and forward, and his present is suspended between a past from which he can become free and a future toward which he is moving. Man has possibilities of growth, the capacity to make decisions or to respond to love. Jesus always saw men in terms of what they truly were and what they could become. The very fact that people go to a pastor at all indicates they have a desire to change and to grow.

5. Man is a social being. The self never exists except in relationship to others. Man can and will respond to love, both the love of God and the love of man. God is ever seeking man's response to His love. (This is demonstrated in the story of the Prodigal Son, the story of the Good Shepherd, in fact, in the entire New Testament.) People also respond to the love of man. This is the only way some can experience or understand the love of God. The pastor can be an agent of redemption through love.

6. Both psychotherapy and pastoral psychology share a concern for man as the object of care and concern. In a pastor's understanding of Man he must include the biblical and theological teachings as well as the findings of the behavorial sciences. All truth is of God.

7. Service to man is an act of faith. Albert Outler said, "Our ultimate confidence is not in ourselves, nor in man or nature, but in God--who has made us for Himself and made us to be ourselves and who will not leave His work unfinished." He maintained that it is through the "divine initiative of love and grace and the intelligent collaboration of faithful and devoted man, . . .(that) human possibilities are fully realized."*

*Psychotherapy and the Christian Message (Harper and Bros., 1954), p. 195.

8. Service to men is service to God. Daniel Day Williams, the noted theologian, asks the question, "Who is this person who comes to the pastor with a burden, a bewilderment, perhaps a flaming hatred?" Then he continues with what he says is a startling answer. For the Christian, "The person is Christ himself standing before the minister." The Christian faith is that Christ is, wherever there is human need, and Williams quotes, "Inasmuch as ye have done it unto one of the least of these my brethren, ye have done it unto me" (Matthew 25:40 KJV). This truth, Dr. Williams says, affects the pastoral relationship profoundly.

FOR FURTHER STUDY: Read on the doctrine of Man in the area of Christian theology. Read on the subject of Personality Theory from the books listed in the Bibliography.

FOR PERSONAL GROWTH: Study all references to man in the Scripture and write out your own doctrine of Man as it relates to pastoral counseling and pastoral care.

RELATING THEORY TO PRACTICE: Review all recent and current counseling sessions, asking yourself the following questions: What does this person's behavior suggest about the doctrine of Man? Was I consistent with my own theory of the doctrine of Man in relationship to this person?

54. THE HOLY SPIRIT IN PASTORAL COUNSELING

Daniel Day Williams, in his book entitled The Minister and the Care of Souls, said, "To bring salvation to the human spirit is the goal of all Christian ministry and pastoral care."* This statement puts wide dimensions on the pastoral task and points out something that is distinctive and unique about both the goals and resources of pastoral counseling. If the pastor is to minister fully to the human spirit, he must link himself with the Spirit of God, or the Holy Spirit.

The doctrine of the Holy Spirit is one that has caused endless discussion, and on which there is great diversity of opinion. This is not surprising when one considers there are over 150 references to the Holy Spirit in the New Testament alone.

This fact points out the great importance that the New Testament writers as-

*P. 11.

121

cribe to the presence of the Holy Spirit. "For them it was intensely personal and extremely practical." In Alan Richardson's Theological Word Book of the Bible the discussion of the Holy Spirit is summarized with this statement. Through the Spirit, he says, "the life energy of the Eternal has flowed into the lives of the believers. That is the meaning of the power of the Spirit. By this men and women become reconciled to God and are made new creatures."*

The last sentence of the above quotation is a good definition of the goals of pastoral care. Henry Van Dusen, in a thought-provoking book, Spirit, Son and Father, after surveying both the biblical and historical interpretations of the doctrine of the Holy Spirit, also stresses its personal, practical application. In spite of the diversity of interpretation he says, two elements are always present, God's presence and God's activity. "The 'Spirit of God' testifies to the immediately present activity of the Divine--God-near and God-mighty. The 'Spirit of God' or 'Holy Spirit' is always God at hand, and the 'Spirit of God' or 'Holy Spirit' is always God at work."**

How does this apply to the work of the pastor? The following emphases suggest some ways:

1. A function of the ministry is to testify to the presence of the Spirit of God. Any attempt to define it, discuss it, or defend it is subject to what Daniel Day Williams calls the "brokenness" or inadequacy of language.

2. There is no denominational, ecclesiastical, or sectarian agreement about the doctrine of the Holy Spirit. Each pastor and counselee can and must develop his own concept in the light of the truth as he sees it.

3. It is believed that the Spirit of God is present on all occasions, but significantly and uniquely in the counseling relationship, when a person is grappling with the basic issues of life.

4. To speak of the presence of the Spirit does not mean that the Spirit is discussed or even recognized. Religious terms may not be mentioned, but the Spirit is still present.

5. To speak of the Spirit as being present in pastoral counseling does not imply that the Spirit is not present in other forms of so-called secular counseling as well. We believe that the Spirit is present, even when the participants may be unaware of the fact.

6. To recognize the presence of the Spirit and the power of God is not to justify any lessening of effort or evading of responsibility on the part of either pastor or counselee. True, God's Spirit is present, but He works through the efforts of men.

7. One of the goals of pastoral counseling is to help the counselee become conscious of the Spirit and put his trust and efforts in the realization of the power of the Spirit of God. A word of caution is necessary: The manifestations may take many forms, wholesome and neurotic. Sometimes a person may use the idea of the Spirit neurotically.

*P. 246.
**Van Dusen, Spirit, Son and Father (Scribner's, 1958), p. 19.

8. A consciousness of the presence of the Spirit of God can be a source of great reassurance for the pastor. He does not have to play God and accept full responsibility for all his counselees' problems. He is conscious that God is more concerned about them than he is. Therefore he can work both humbly and confidently.

Wayne Oates quotes with approval a statement of the Commission on the Ministry of the New York Academy of Sciences. "The clergyman always sees God as a partner in the counseling process. . . and feels rather hesitant in attributing to his own efforts whatever success may be achieved." Then Dr. Oates goes further and says, "The spiritually secure pastor knows that the life of the counselee is actually in the hands of God, and not his. The Holy Spirit and not he himself is the Counselor."* This consciousness does not lessen the counselor's sense of responsibility to the counselee, but puts it into a larger context of meaning.

9. The affirmation of the presence of the Spirit is a source of guidance and strength not only to the counselee, but also to the pastoral counselor. He doesn't have to have all the answers. He too has feelings of discouragement, isolation, and frustration. He too needs to become a new person, needs the assurance of forgiveness and a consciousness of the power of the Spirit in order that he can serve. The Spirit of God is his great resource and assurance of strength.

10. Admittedly we are dealing with a mystery, a reality too great for finite minds to grasp, but a reality that many have and all may experience. Those who have, testify to its very real, meaningful and significant results.

"For where two or three are gathered in my name, there am I in the midst of them." (Matthew 18:20.)

"But the fruit of the Spirit is love, joy, peace, patience, kindness, goodness, faithfulness, gentleness, self-control; against such there is no law." (Galatians 5:22.)

". . .that according to the riches of his glory he may grant you to be strengthened with might through his Spirit in the inner man, and that Christ may dwell in your hearts through faith; that you, being rooted and grounded in love, may have power to comprehend with all the saints what is the breadth and length and height and depth, and to know the love of Christ which surpasses knowledge, that you may be filled with all the fulness of God." (Ephesians 3:16-19.)

FOR FURTHER STUDY: Read the passages in both the Old and New Testament related to the Holy Spirit. Read interpretations of Christian thought about the Holy Spirit.

FOR PERSONAL GROWTH: Write out your own doctrine of the Holy Spirit as it relates to counseling and pastoral care.

*Oates, Protestant Pastoral Counseling, pp. 58, 59.

55. WHAT IS UNIQUE ABOUT PASTORAL COUNSELING?

Counseling like public speaking crosses many professional lines. Doctors, lawyers, teachers, psychologists, and social workers all do counseling. It should be apparent that there are many similarities in all types of counseling. There are many principles that apply to counseling, pastoral or otherwise. This is as it should be. Much of what the pastoral counselor does is the same as what any other counselor does. What are the differences? What is unique about pastoral counseling?

1. One major difference is the symbolic role of the pastor. All professional people--the doctor, the psychiatrist, the social worker--have symbolic roles. These can be either negative or positive in their influence. The attitudes of people toward the pastor differ from their attitudes toward other professions. The pastor represents something far beyond himself. He represents religion. He represents the church. He represents God.

2. The pastoral setting is different. Hiltner and Colston in their study The Context of Pastoral Counseling found that people go to a church with different attitudes from those with which they go to a hospital, a clinic, a library, or a social agency. What attitudes people bring to a pastoral counseling center are not known for sure, but that they are influential on their behavior there can be no doubt.

3. The pastor can initiate a relationship. This is one value of the pastoral call. The pastor has access to homes and hospitals, etc., by viture of his position. This is more true in the parish setting than at a counseling center.

4. The pastor's training is different from that of any other counselor. One's training has a strong influence on how he looks at a person, sees a situation, evaluates issues as to their importance and determines procedures he will follow. The pastor is trained as a theologian, a biblical scholar, and as a pastor. Thus he sees things from the perspective of his doctrine of man and his understanding of religious truth.

5. Because of his role in the community, a pastor is considered a specialist in some areas. These include such things as premarital counseling, ministering to the sorrowing, dealing with problems of religious doubt or guilt, and counseling those considering church vocations.

6. The pastor by training and by role can utilize religious resources (see Section 39).

7. The pastor performs other functions parallel or supplementary to counseling, such as preaching, worship, leading service groups, etc. This is more true of the pastor in the parish than in a counseling center.

8. The pastor has a continuing relationship with a person that began before the immediate problem and continues after it is resolved. This gives him a background of knowledge about the person and an opportunity for follow-up. Again, this is more true in the parish than at a center, and is one reason that a counseling center must maintain a close relationship with the pastors of the counselees. A pastor at a pastoral counseling center has some advantages in that he does not have a continuing relationship. He will not see the person at church activities, therefore the person may find it easier to talk to him frankly and personally.

FOR FURTHER STUDY: Read extensively the material on pastoral care listed in the Bibliography.

FOR PERSONAL GROWTH: Write out in your own words three things that you feel distinguish pastoral counseling from general counseling. Prepare your own statement of what you feel is unique about pastoral counseling.

Appendices

APPENDIX 1: THE PASTORAL CARE AND TRAINING CENTER

The Pastoral Care and Training Center began its operation in the fall of 1968 as a part of the training program in pastoral care of Brite Divinity School. The title, while a bit awkward, was chosen with considerable care. "Pastoral Care" was selected because it is a pastoral service and the term "care" has a broader connotation than "counseling." The word "training" is included because it is a training center. Its stated purposes were three:

1. To provide advanced training in pastoral care.
2. To render a service to the people and the churches of the Fort Worth community.
3. To provide a basis for furthering research and study of pastoral care and counseling.

The first two have been done from the beginning. The third, research and study of pastoral care procedures, has been done only in part, although many possibilities in these areas exist and some projects are in process.

Before the Center began its operation certain principles or guidelines were established.

1. The program was to be pastoral in nature. There was no intention of its becoming another mental health clinic or of duplicating other agencies.

2. The program would be completely ecumenical, both interdenominational and interfaith.

3. Adequate psychiatric consultation and supervision would be maintained at all times.

4. An advisory committee representing all of the helping professions--medicine, law, social work, education, psychology, and psychiatry--would shape the policies of the program, and constant communication and consultation would be maintained with specialists in these fields when it is indicated.

5. All persons serving as counselors in the Center would be carefully screened and selected because of their academic training, personal qualifications, and experience.

6. The counselors working in the Center would receive careful supervision, both pastoral and psychiatric. This is done individually and in groups. The purposes are to render a more responsible service to those coming for help, and to provide personal and intense training.

The services provided by the Center are all basically pastoral in nature but they have covered a rather wide range of human need. Most extensive has been the pastoral counseling provided to persons who have come to the Center itself. Most of these persons have been referred by pastors and physicians, although many come by self-referral. In the second and third years of operation a large proportion came because they had talked to others who had been here. Since the Center is located within a block of a University, many students have come for counseling.

It has been the policy from the beginning that pastoral care services would also be provided in the poverty area, and for persons who would find it difficult--for either practical or psychological reasons--to come to the Center. Consequently counselors have been located in the poverty area; chaplaincy services have been provided in the county hospital; group counseling has been made available to homes for unwed mothers and other agencies.

The response from the community has been good. Thirty-three persons sought assistance the first month, 58 the second, 58 the third. During the first 12 months an average of 47 new people came each month. During the first 12 months, 524 persons were seen in one capacity or another and more than 1700 interviews were conducted. At the present time, approximately 60 people are seen each week, which is the maximum that can be handled by the present staff.

Some of these persons are seen once and referred to a psychiatrist or some other agency. Some are seen extensively for weeks or months. A check of addresses indicates people have come from every part of the community and from 22 surrounding towns. Some travel as much as 100 to 150 miles for counseling. They represent every religious affiliation and none at all.

Certain observations may be drawn from the experience at the Pastoral Care and Training Center thus far. There is nothing new about them. Most of them have been known for a long time. The experience thus far has simply served to highlight them, to emphasize them, to put them in a bit sharper focus.

1. Human need is everywhere. It exists in every community, whether rural or urban. It is present in every part of the community--in the inner city, in the suburbs, in the ghetto, and on the campus. It is present among the rich and the poor, the wise and the simple, the scholar and the unskilled laborer. John Watson was right when he said, "Be kind, everyone you meet is fighting a hard battle."

2. People do think of the pastor, the church, or religious agencies when they need help. Some come hesitantly, some reluctantly, some hopefully, but they do turn to the church and its ministry in great numbers.

3. The church must meet these needs more effectively. It has been pointed out that the church is in a state of transition; some say it is out-of-date, even irrelevant. What the future form of the church will be, we do not know, but some means of helping resolve man's deep and pressing concerns must be preserved and improved. When the church is involved in the struggle of persons it is not irrelevant.

4. A more effective ministry must be trained. This includes all pastors, for all are faced with this problem. It includes some who must be trained as specialists to serve in multiple staffs with a major responsibility for pastoral care, some who can serve in a specialized way in institutions, some who can teach and supervise in seminaries and pastoral care centers.

New forms of training must be developed. The value of a clinical approach to theological education has been evident since the pioneer work of Dicks and Boisen. Much improvement needs to take place. Pastoral care must have a closer relationship with the theological disciplines on the one hand and the behavioral sciences on the other. It must include an understanding of and experience with the normative and maladjusted, with those in institutions, and those in the community. New forms of supervision that are interdisciplinary in nature must be developed.

5. Cooperation with the other healing and helping professions is both a possibility and a necessity. Our experience has taught us how helpful this can be and how important it is. The whole trend toward community mental health centers and toward closer cooperation between all professions gives the pastor a great opportunity and a new responsibility.

6. Pastoral counseling and pastoral care can produce results. This has been true for centuries. With new methods and deeper understanding even greater results can be expected. Success is difficult to measure. Spectacular results may appear and fade, the evidence of some results may not appear for years, but healing, growth, integration, and salvation can and do occur.

APPENDIX 2: HANDBOOK FOR COUNSELEES

This material was prepared for those who come to the Center for counseling. It is available in pamphlet form and given to each person who comes to the Center. Its purpose is to help them understand the nature of pastoral counseling and how they can use the services most helpfully.

A GUIDE FOR THOSE WHO COME TO
THE PASTORAL CARE AND COUNSELING CENTER

The Pastoral Care and Training Center was established in the fall of 1968 to provide pastoral counseling to persons of this area and advanced training in pastoral care to graduate students in Brite Divinity School.

This brochure is prepared to inform you of the nature of the services available, the principles on which the Center operates, and to help those who wish to utilize the services of the Center understand how they can use them most effectively.

The material is put in question and answer form because that is the way they often come to us. If you have further questions, feel free to raise them with any member of the staff.

What are the purposes of the Center?
As stated in the introductory paragraph the purposes are two: one is to provide pastoral counseling in personal, social, or spiritual problems; the other is to provide advanced training in pastoral counseling and pastoral care.

What is pastoral counseling?
Pastoral counseling is a method by which a clergyman seeks to help another person cope with a personal, social, or religious problem.

What are the basic premises of pastoral counseling?
Pastoral counseling is based on certain general convictions, which have been demonstrated repeatedly. One is the conviction that problems can be coped with, decisions can be reached, growth can take place.

Another is that persons have the capacity to grow, to mature, to understand. At times it takes some effort to release this capacity but it is our confidence that the capacity is there.

A third conviction is that the counseling process is effective, that pastors can help in the difficult task of living a more effective life.

A fourth conviction is that God is in the process. Just as the healing power of nature produces healing when a doctor dresses a wound, so the healing power of God is present when a person is striving to understand, to cope with his troubles, to overcome his guilt, to be a better and stronger person.

132

The following questions have been raised by many people during or after counseling. Some of them may be of interest to you.

Is this something new?
No. This is as old as the scripture. The concept of the religious leader as one who served the people appears clear back in the shepherding concept of the Old Testament. The word "pastor" means "one who serves." Most of the ministry of Jesus was to individuals who came to Him for help.
Pastors have been doing this for generations. It is as old as the ministry. Richard Baxter, Horace Bushnell, Phillips Brooks were excellent counselors long before there were such terms as pastoral psychology, or pastoral counseling. Brooks's biographer said, "his house was a refuge for all who were in trouble." John Frederic Oberlin couldn't resist the cry of the needy. Pastors have always tried to help persons with their needs and problems. Furthermore, these men of a previous generation were very effective.

What is new about pastoral counseling?
Pastors today can combine the age-old wisdom of the scripture with the findings of psychology, psychotherapy, and mental hygiene. This does not give them a new task. It provides new understandings of human behavior and new methods and techniques of helping persons who need their help.

Who are the counselors?
The counseling is done by postgraduate students in Brite Divinity School and the faculty members of the Department of Pastoral Care in Brite Divinity School.

What training have the counselors had?
All counselors on the staff of the Center have completed a college degree and a graduate degree in theological seminary. This consists of a minimum of three years above an AB, and includes all the general training a qualified pastor would receive, such as biblical, theological, and historical studies. Also it includes a basic understanding of human behavior, the principles and procedures of counseling, the relationship of the Christian faith to human need, and, in most cases, supervised pastoral experience in a hospital, a counseling center, or some other clinical setting. All the counselors in the Center either have completed or are engaged in postgraduate studies in pastoral counseling.

How is the program supervised?
The work of all counselors is closely supervised by the staff of the Department of Pastoral Care of Brite Divinity School, and by Dr. Robert Glen of the Department of Psychiatry of Southwestern Medical School of the University of Texas. In addition to the direct supervision of the counselors an interdisciplinary advisory committee, representing such fields as psychiatry, medicine, social work, law, etc., guides and directs the policies of the program.

What kinds of problems are brought to the Pastoral Care and Training Center?
One might answer this by saying "all kinds." Problems are so interrelated it is difficult to classify or categorize them. Perhaps the most frequent are family problems, but there are also problems of personal adjustment, discouragement, doubt, guilt, etc.

What are the limitations of pastoral counseling?
The pastor functions as a pastor. He is not trained as a doctor, psychiatrist, psychometrist, lawyer, or social worker. One should not expect him to be. When he is presented with problems in any of these areas, he rightfully refers.

What is the relationship to other counseling and mental health services in the community?
The Pastoral Care Center maintains a close relationship with the other agencies in the area. It does not attempt to compete with or duplicate services that can be secured in other counseling agencies.

What does the staff at the Center do if it feels the problem is not one with which it should deal?
If there are indications that some other specialist should be utilized, the counselor will say so. We do not attempt to do what others are more qualified to do. If it seems that a psychiatrist, a physician, a psychologist, a social worker, an attorney, or an agency such as the Family Service Association should be used, the person will be told so and, if need be, helped to make contact with such a service.

Is a medical examination necessary?
It is not a requirement for being admitted to the program of the Center but it is strongly recommended. When any physical symptoms are present, the Center does insist on a medical diagnosis and, if need be, treatment. It is essential that the physical components of a problem be dealt with from a medical point of view in order that the psychological and spiritual elements can be dealt with by the staff of the Center.

Is the program denominational?
No. The staff represents several denominations and the persons who come for help represent all religious groups. It is completely ecumenical, both interdenominational and interfaith.

Do counselors at the Center take the place of local pastors?
In no wise. We attempt to provide services for those persons who may or may not have a pastor, or for those persons whose pastor may feel we can render additional help. The Pastoral Care and Training Center is not a church, does not conduct preaching or the sacraments. It encourages people to participate in their own church as actively as they wish. It supplements the work of the church by providing counseling services for its members.

Is counseling confidential?
Yes. We hold to this very strictly. Wayne Oates calls it a "covenant of communication." What is discussed in the counseling sessions will be held in strict confidence by both parties unless permission is given for it to be repeated, or unless the person is told what is being done.

What are the financial arrangements?
Payment for services is arranged on a basis of one's willingness or capacity to contribute. It has been proved that it is not good to receive help without contributing something in return. There is no standard fee. In fact each person sets his own fee. This can be worked out with the director. No one need feel any embarrassment, no one will be refused because of inability to pay. However, the Center depends in part upon the contributions of those who receive its benefits.

Is there any way one who cannot pay can render a service in return?
Yes. It is a proven fact that people who have received benefits of a service will be stronger if they do something for someone else. There are a few volunteer tasks that can be done at the Center; however, it is just as important that a person find something he can do for someone else anywhere, a neighbor, a friend, a member of his family, his church, some community cause. We repeat, he who receives should give—in some way.

Are psychological tests used?
Yes, when indicated. When a test or battery of tests will help the counselor understand the person's needs better, he will recommend them. Some of these tests can be administered at the Center, some can be taken at the TCU testing center (for a modest fee), or they can be secured from a clinical psychologist.

What information is secured from tests?
Each test is designed for a specific purpose. Some measure mental ability or scholastic aptitude; some measure vocational interests, others vocational aptitude; some measure educational achievement; and some give an understanding of a person's emotional adjustment. These are clues which help the counselor understand the person's needs, but--more important--help the person understand himself.

Are test findings confidential?
Yes. This information will not be released to anyone outside the Center without the person's consent.

Does all of the counseling take place at the Center?
No. Counseling programs are also conducted in the poverty area and programs of group counseling are held in social agencies.

Is group counseling available?
There are limited opportunities for participation in groups.

How does one feel when coming for counseling?

If your reactions are similar to most, you have a combination of many feelings. Most people came for counseling with great hesitation, considerable embarrassment, much uncertainty. Some are apologetic, feeling that to ask for help is a sign of weakness or an indication of immaturity. Actually, the opposite is true. To recognize one's need is a sign of maturity and strength. Many who have never been counseled before wonder what will happen, what they should say, whether or not they will be preached to. Some even have a bit of hostility. They resent having to seek help and may unconsciously feel angry toward the one from whom they are seeking help. Such feelings are quite normal, and should be expected.

How long will it take?

No one really knows. Very simple problems can be solved in a few interviews. Most problems take longer. Sometimes it takes many interviews. It all depends on the nature of the problem, how complicated are the issues, how many people are involved, how well motivated the counselee is, etc. The important thing is the that both counselee and counselor see it through to a conclusion.

How long should an interview be?

There is no standard time for an interview. The traditional length is fifty minutes or an hour. Whether this is due to the fact that classes, television programs, etc., last an hour, we do not know. It does seem that maximum benefits are usually achieved within 30 to 50 minutes. When possible, it is usually better to break it up into two or three interviews rather than one long session of several hours. Circumstances alter cases. Some days an hour doesn't seem long enough, but on other days ten minutes is adequate.

Where should I begin?

Many, many people ask this question. It is a natural question. It is not easy to know where to start. Usually problems are so complex that many things are on one's mind. The best place to begin is where it seems most natural. The things to discuss are the things that are causing the most trouble. As you proceed you will get most of the relevant concerns.

What is meant by the phrase "Counseling is helping people help themselves"?

No one can live another's life for him. He couldn't if he would, and shouldn't if he could. No one can really make another's decisions for him. At times it is necessary to have help. During great stress another may be of great assistance, but even then he does not take over the other person's life. The counselor's task is to help a person understand himself, to weigh all the alternatives and make his own decisions, to stand on his own feet, to live his own life. To make decisions for another, to protect him unnecessarily is not good for either the counselor or the person. The counselor's task is to make himself increasingly unnecessary.

Does anyone have problems like mine?
Many people feel this way. Some frankly ask, "Have you ever known anyone who is as messed up as I am?" The answer is simply, "Yes, many." While each person's problem is unique, yet problems are almost universal. As one man put it—whatever your problem you can be sure five thousand people have one just like it. A study of either the Bible or biography makes it quite clear, even the great personalities had problems too.

Does everyone feel anxious and inadequate?
Everyone has some anxieties, probably everyone feels inadequate at times. This is not necessarily bad. It may have very positive results. Anxiety or inadequacy feelings are bad when they are never relieved; when they are crippling, when they keep us from enjoying life or performing at our best.

"Can I ever be forgiven?"
Many people suffer from guilt. Probably everyone does at some time or other. It is the central teaching of the Christian faith that forgiveness is available if one fulfills the condition.

Why is counseling so difficult?
There is no magic in counseling. It is hard work, time consuming, on occasion embarrassing and sometimes painful. In fact, if no difficulty is encountered, little progress will usually take place. After all, counseling deals with some of the most troubling but significant aspects of experience. We would not expect it to be easy—but it is worth it.

Does pastoral counseling really work?
Many people wonder about this. They come almost as a last resort but really wonder whether or not it will do any good. Some frankly say so, or ask the question stated above. Success, of course, is relative and depends on many things. However, it can be said with great assurance, and it is testified to by literally thousands of cases, that people have been helped by the pastoral counseling process. It means the person must accept certain responsibilities, make certain efforts, but when he does, results do take place.
It has been demonstrated that problems can be solved, decisions can be made, personal and spiritual growth can take place.

When does religion enter the process?
Some have specific and definite religious problems. These may be the center of focus. Because of his religious orientation the pastoral counselor can usually help in such areas.
However, in another sense, religion enters in whether religious words or ideas are ever mentioned. It is the conviction of the staff that God is both involved and concerned whenever a person makes an honest effort to face himself, to understand others, to recognize his weaknesses and build up his strengths; and that this is a sacred and spiritual matter and is very much a religious commitment.

Does just talking help?

Many ask this question. We would point out that "just" talking is never done. It is a planned approach of facing life situations, and talking about it does produce results. It has been demonstrated many times that talking does lower anxiety, relieve tension, and often lead to new insights.

In working with the counselor should I talk about what has happened in the past, or the future?

Probably both. We are all a product of the past and the better we understand it the better off we are. Also our hopes and plans for the future must be faced as well.

Is progress continuous?

No. We wish it were, but it is only realistic to recognize that growth takes place unevenly. There come new insights, new advances. One reaches plateaus and there are occasional setbacks. This is the test. Both counselor and counselee regroup their forces and continue.

How can I (the counselee) help the counseling process?

As much depends on the attitude of the counselee as on the skill of the counselor. Your desire to attain wholeness to resolve the problem is basic and all important. There is an axiom in all such work that you can only help those who desire to be helped.

Remember you must do most of the talking. It is only as you express your true feelings that the counselor can understand. It has been demonstrated countless times that as you do so you gain new insights.

Don't expect magic or miracles. The pastoral counselor is a counselor, not a magician, miracle worker, or a fortune-teller. He uses procedures that have been proven to be helpful, but there are no magic or quick solutions.

Persistence and patience are all important. Most problems have developed over a long period of time. It is only to be expected they will take time to reach a solution. Often when one seems most confused or discouraged, he may be near a new insight or understanding. It does take time, but how could you invest your time in anything more important?

Recognize that this is hard work, sometimes painful—but worth it. Nothing is more important than self-understanding, growth, and faith.

Recognize that you must accept responsibility for your own life; ultimately you must make your own decisions, put into practice the insights gained through counseling.

What can I do outside of counseling that will help?

Certain activities--tension-reducing techniques that are done parallel to counseling--may be just as important as the counseling itself. Not all these apply to every person, but most of them, or some combination of them will be helpful in most cases.

1. Make a rather careful evaluation of your time and how you are using your energy. In most cases it is well to simplify and develop some orderly, systematic program. Eliminate that which is unnecessary. Give priority to those things that are of most value.

2. Cultivate the capacity to relax. This is all important in cases where tension is present. You can't be tense and relaxed at the same time. It is physically and psychologically impossible. Cultivate the ability to relax. Spend at least 15 to 30 minutes a day in complete relaxation. Reading a book like Jacobson's You Must Relax may help you with the concept, although you probably don't need to follow all of his procedures. The important thing is to get the feel of relaxation and when you feel tense, learn to relax. Do not expect immediate results, but begin the program now.

3. Do some physical exercise every day unless it is impossible to do so. There is a close relationship between tension and physical states. One can work off much tension by physical activity. Walk around the block, do sitting-up exercises, work in the yard, but spend some time in physical activity every day.

4. Pay attention to your hobbies. Cultivate some if you have none. Everyone should have some things he does merely because he likes to do them—and for no other reason. This cannot always be done regularly but, if possible, spend some time every week in such pleasure.

5. Do some free writing. There is evidence to show that simply writing one's thought on paper may help. This should be quite spontaneous; pay no attention to penmanship, punctuation, grammar; just let yourself go. Tear it up if you would not want someone to see it, or bring it to the next interview.

6. Do some inspirational reading. Man not only has the capacity to do evil, he also has the capacity to be inspired. Some like to read better than others. The time need not be lengthy. It may be only a few minutes, but it is well to feed our minds and spirits with great thoughts, inspirational ideas. What appeals to one may not to another. The thing to do is find that which speaks to you. This should not be seen as an assignment, but as an opportunity.

7. Cultivate the capacity to see the positive, life-giving elements in a situation. This does not mean a superficial evasion of evil, or false positive thinking. It must take into full account the facts but also recognize that in every situation there are positive elements. Think of the things for which you should be grateful and of which you can be proud.

8. Spend some time each day in prayer. This is not the place to argue prayer. There is such a place, but that is not our concern here. It is good to seek more understanding, but one does not have to be able to resolve all of the intellectual difficulties to be able to appropriate the values of prayer and worship. We recognize that for many people confession, petition, intercession, thanksgiving and praise, commitment, and dedication have been of inestimable value. Appropriate as much of this as you possibly can—sincerely and regularly.

9. Live by faith. Again this may be difficult for some. They do not feel they have faith. This is not the time to debate it. There is such a time. In the meantime,

make it an adventure. As the man in the Gospels said, "I believe, help thou my unbelief."

10. Do something for someone else. This is all important. It does not need to be spectacular or unusual. It may be very simple—write a letter, mow a yard, give a word of encouragement, but do something; the more you can do, the better.

APPENDIX 3: RECORD BLANKS

This section includes the record blanks used at the Pastoral Care and Training Center. They consist of information received on the intake interview, permission blanks for consultation, the counseling record forms for the confidential file, and a monthly progress report each counselor turns in on his counselees. This later report is designed for the computer in order that research on pastoral care can be conducted much more thoroughly.

CONFIDENTIAL INFORMATION SHEET

This information is to help us understand you and your situation and help you better. Please fill it out as completely as you can. All information will be held in strict confidence.

Name _____
         Last   First   Middle

Phone Number (at home) _____ (at work) _____

Address _____

Age _____ Sex _____

Marital Status _____ Length of time _____

Is this your only marriage? _____ If not, please list dates.

_____

Place in the family. List your brothers by (M) and sisters by (F) from the oldest on the left to the youngest on the right. Include yourself and circle the one which is you.

_____

State briefly your relationship with your brothers and sisters.

_____
_____
_____
_____
_____

Parents occupation:

Father: _____ Living _____ (If deceased, give date)

_____

Mother: _____ Living _____ (If deceased, give date)

_____
Where do your parents live? Father _____ Mother _____

Were your parents separated or divorced? If so, indicate your age when the separation occurred. _____

State briefly your relationship with your parents.

_____
_____
_____
_____

List children from this and/or previous marriages.

Name   Sex Date of Birth Place of Residence

_____
_____
_____
_____

Church Affiliation _____
  Pastor's name _____
Have you ever belonged to other denominations? _____
If so, please list them. _____

Do you find your religion satisfying ____, challenging ____, meaningless ____,
dull ____, irrelevant ____?
Please state briefly the nature of your religious experience.

_____
_____
_____
_____

Education: Please list the schools attended and degrees granted.

  School   Degree   Date

_____
_____

College Major _____ College Grade Average _____
Vocational Experience (Please list the positions you have held and number of years
spent in each. List your present occupation on the top line.)

  Position   Years

_____
_____
_____
_____
_____

Do you enjoy your present occupation? ____
Would you like to change? ____
If so, what would you prefer? ____
What is the general condition of your health? _____
Do you have any physical disabilities that would be pertinent to your problem? ____
If yes, please indicate their nature.

_____

Are you under the care of a physician? _____
    His name _____
State in your own words the nature of the problem you wish to discuss.

_____

_____

_____

Give a brief account of the history or length of duration of the problem.

_____

_____

_____

_____

Have you consulted anyone else about this problem? _____
If the answer is yes, indicate who. _____
Would you be willing for us to discuss it with him? _____
Who referred you to the Pastoral Care Center? _____
Would you be willing to take a battery of psychological tests? _____
Would you be willing to consult a physician if it is indicated? _____
Would you be willing to have your situation discussed by the staff of the Center, with the assurance it will not be discussed outside the professional staff? _____

CONSENT FOR CONSULTATION

    I (we) hereby authorize the Brite Pastoral Care and Training Center to consult with the persons listed below as it is deemed necessary to assist in counseling with me (us). I (we) hereby waive the privilege of confidential communication between pastor, physician, or other professional for these purposes. It is my understanding that it is only for this purpose and any information received will be held in strict confidence by the Center.

	Name	Address	Phone
1. Pastor			
2. Physician			
3. Attorney			
4. Social Agency			
5. School Counselor or others			

Date _____   Signed _____

PERMISSION FOR CONSULTATION

It is my understanding that material from my interviews will be discussed with my counselor's supervisors. All information will be handled professionally and confidentially. It is my understanding that the purpose is to enable him to render a better service to me and increase his effectiveness with others. I hereby grant such permission.

Date _____   Signed _____

PERMISSION FOR PROFESSIONAL INFORMATION

Date _____

Dear _____:

    I (we) hereby grant permission that you share any information about me (us) with the Brite Pastoral Care and Training Center that will be helpful in their counseling with us.

Sincerely,

_____

PERMISSION FOR CASE CONFERENCE

It is my understanding that material from my interviews may be used in a case conference. The purpose would be to help my counselor help me and as a source of training to benefit others who are in training. All material would be handled professionally and confidentially within this context. I hereby grant permission for such use.

Date _____   Signed _____

Pastoral Counseling Records
(Keep in locked file)

Interview Summary

Name _____ Date _____ Time _____

1. Observations (counselee's appearance, nonverbal behavior, feeling)

2. Summary of what transpired in the interview.

3. Significant feelings expressed

Procedural plans, recommendations, interpretation, etc.

Counselor's evaluation

Counselor's signature _____

Supervisor's comments

Supervisor's signature _____

PASTORAL COUNSELING CENTER

Termination Interview

Counselee: Supervisor:
Counselor: Date:

146

I. Brief description of final interview and events leading to termination:

II. Total number of interviews including final interview.
III. Reasons for termination:
    A. How was termination initiated?
        _____ 1. Termination was by mutual consent.
        _____ 2. Counselee initiated termination.
        _____ 3. Counselor initiated termination.
        _____ 4. Counselee did not return.
    B. Describe the counselee's verbalized reason for termination.

    C. What was the counselor's impression of the real reason for termination?

    D. Was termination at this time appropriate? Explain.

IV. A. Was counselee referred to another counselor or agency? If so, to whom?

    B. Briefly summarize communication with counselor or agency to whom referred.

PASTORAL CARE CENTER

MONTHLY PROGRESS REPORT

DATE: |1|2|3|4|5|6|

|1|2|3|4|5|6|7|8|9|0|1|2|3|4|5|6|7|8|9|0| |1|2|3|4|

COUNSELEE: └────────────────────┘ NO. └────┘

(LAST, FIRST, INITIAL)

|1|2|3|4|5|6|7|8|9|0|1|2|3|4|5|6|7|8|9|0| |1|2|3|4|

COUNSELOR: └────────────────────┘ NO. └────┘

NUMBER OF SESSIONS TO DATE: └────┘
        THIS MONTH   : └──┘ |1|2|3|4|5|6|7|8|9|0|1|2|3|4|5|6|7|8|
        MISSED   : └──┘ REASON: └────────────────┘   01

COUNSELEE'S RESPONSE TO COUNSELING:

1. GENERAL PROGRESS TO DATE   ( ) EXCELLENT
                                   ( ) SATISFACTORY
                                   ( ) POOR

2. SYMPTOMS: ( ) BETTER
                                   ( ) THE SAME
                                   ( ) WORSE

3. APPOINTMENTS: ( ) COMES ON TIME
                                   ( ) COMES EARLY
                                   ( ) COMES LATE

4. COMMUNICATIVENESS: ( ) SATISFACTORY
                                   ( ) OVERPRODUCTIVE
                                   ( ) INCOHERENT
                                   ( ) LONG PERIODS OF SILENCE
                                   ( ) OTHER- |1|2|3|4|5|6|7|8|9|0|1|2|3|4|5|
                                              └────────────────┘

5. RELATIONSHIP WITH COUNSELOR: ( ) GOOD
                                   ( ) FAIR
                                   ( ) POOR
                                   ( ) INTENSE DEPENDENCY
                                   ( ) SEXUAL FEELINGS
                                   ( ) FEAR
                                   ( ) DETACHMENT
                                   ( ) NEGATIVISM
                                   ( ) HOSTILITY
                                   ( ) OTHER- |1|2|3|4|5|6|7|8|9|0|1|2|3|4|
                                              └────────────────┘

148

6. RESISTANCE: ( ) LOW
                                        ( ) MODERATE
                                        ( ) STRONG
                                        ( ) INTERFERES WITH PROGRESS
                                        ( ) ACTING OUT TENDENCIES

7. INSIGHT: ( ) ACHIEVING INSIGHT
                                        ( ) CURIOSITY ABOUT DYNAMICS
                                        ( ) INTELLECTUAL, BUT NO EMOTIONAL
                                            INSIGHT
                                        ( ) RESISTS INSIGHT

8. TRANSLATION OF INSIGHTS INTO ACTION: ( ) EXCELLENT
                                        ( ) SATISFACTORY
                                        ( ) POOR

9. SEVERE ENVIRONMENTAL PROBLEMS: ( ) FINANCES
                                        ( ) WORK
                                        ( ) FAMILY
                                        ( ) OTHER- 123456789012345

10. REFERRAL: ( ) POSSIBLE
                                        ( ) URGENT
                                        ( ) NO INDICATION
                    if to be referred, ( ) PHYSICIAN
                                        ( ) PSYCHIATRIST
                                        ( ) PSYCHOLOGIST
                                        ( ) FAMILY SERVICE
                                        ( ) OTHER- 123456789012 34

11. TERMINATION: ( ) OVERDUE
                                        ( ) SOON
                                        ( ) NOT FOR LONG TIME
                                        ( ) COUNSELEE WANTS TO DISCONTINUE
                                            BUT PREMATURE

12. METHODS USED:

    SUPPORT   ( ) EFFECTIVE ( ) INEFFECTIVE
    REASSURANCE   ( )   "   ( )   "
    PROBING   ( )   "   ( )   "
    REFLECTIONS OF
        FEELINGS   ( )   "   ( )   "
    RELIGIOUS RESOURCES ( )   "   ( )   "
    CONFRONTATION   ( )   "   ( )   "

13. REMARKS:

    A. NEED OF CONFERENCE: ( ) SUPERVISORY CONFERENCE NEEDED
                                        ( ) EMERGENCY FORESEEN
                                        ( ) DYNAMICS NOT CLEAR
                                        ( ) COUNSELING GOING POORLY

149

(13. A. NEED OF CONFERENCE, CONTINUED) ( ) COUNSELEE WANTS TO DISCONTINUE
( ) COUNSELOR CONSIDERING CLOSING
( ) OTHER- 1 2 3 4 5 6 7 8 9 0 1 2 3 4 5

B. NEED OF CONSULTATION:

( ) CONSULTATION NEEDED
( ) WITH PSYCHIATRIC CONSULTANT
( ) WITH CASEWORKER
( ) WITH PSYCHOLOGIST
( ) WITH MEDICAL CONSULTANT
( ) OTHER- 1 2 3 4 5 6 7 8 9 0 1 2 3 4

04

C. NATURE OF PROBLEM:

( ) SAME AS INTAKE
( ) MORE SEVERE THAN ANTICIPATED
( ) DIFFERENT THAN AT INTAKE
( ) UNCLEAR

1 2 3 4 5 6 7 8 9 0 1 2 3 4 5 6 7 8 9 0 1 2 3 4 5 6 7 8 9 0 1 2 3 4 5 6 7 8 9 0 1 2 3 4 5 6 7 8 9 0 1 2 3 4 5 6 7 8 9 0 1 2

LAST MONTH COUNSELING RESUME   05

06

07

08

09

10

11

12

13

14

15

16

17

18

19

20

21

22

23

24

APPENDIX 4: MEMO TO THE COUNSELORS OF THE PASTORAL CARE AND TRAINING CENTER: THE PROCESS OF SUPERVISION

Supervision is the key to growth in professional skills and effectiveness. There is no other method whereby a person can more effectively relate theory and practice, evaluate himself, and gain an understanding of persons than through individual and group supervision of the pastoral counseling process.

Through supervision one both grows professionally and renders a better service to his counselees simultaneously.

Through supervision one relates his general theological training, his knowledge of classical disciplines to the needs of persons and thus gains a deeper understanding of both.

Through supervision one is able to relate his theoretical knowledge of personality theory and counseling techniques to actual persons and their needs.

Through supervision one works through some of his own feelings and concerns. Supervision is not therapy and should not be considered as such, although through supervision one often gains a great deal of self-understanding and experiences personal growth.

Supervision at the Pastoral Care and Training Center contains both individual and group supervision. The supervision is interdisciplinary in nature and includes three pastoral supervisors, a psychiatric supervisor, and the use of those from other disciplines, such as social work, psychometrics, law, etc., when it is indicated. Whether supervision is done in small groups or with the entire staff, one learns from his fellow students (pastors) as well as from the supervisor.

There are several emphases or areas that should be included in all supervision. Some sessions will concentrate on one aspect, some on another. The particular focus of any one session will be determined primarily by the student. It may include one emphasis or it may include several. The following guidelines should be in the minds of both student and supervisor as goals and purposes of supervision.

1. The focus is on the parishioner (patient, counselee) and his needs. The purpose is to understand this person, what his needs are, how he can be helped, what can be learned from him.

2. The focus is on the counselor (pastor) and his needs. Here the primary emphasis is on the counselor and why he feels as he does toward persons in the pastoral role, in the presence of stress, etc. It considers his hesitations, his anxieties, his feelings of inadequacy, his dependency, as the case may be.

3. The focus is on the methodology or techniques of pastoral counseling or pastoral care. Here the emphasis is on the procedures the counselor used, or should have used, and why. The discussion centers around the use of listening, reflection, interpretation, diagnosis, religious resources, etc. How did the techniques affect the relationship, what was their effectiveness, etc.?

4. The focus is on the relationship between the counselor and the parishioner. This is similar to and includes items 1 and 2, but is sufficiently different to warrant a separation item. Here the discussion centers around the transaction that is taking place, the meaning of the relationship, etc.

5. The focus is on the religious and theological implications of what has taken place. Here the emphasis is on whether the student (pastor) can relate his training in the biblical, theological, and historical fields to actual human need and the work of the pastor.

In order to benefit most from supervisory sessions one should have all information available prior to the session. This would include intake information, interview notes, tapes of sessions, etc. Since tapes can be very time-consuming, they should be edited so that only the most relevant portions of the interview are used.

Supervision does not mean that one must always agree with the supervisor. It does mean that one evaluates all facets of the material and is open to the supervisor's evaluations and suggestions.

The process of supervision is more easily arranged in a training center. However, a pastor or a group of pastors in the community could arrange with a psychologist, a psychiatrist, or a person trained in Clinical Pastoral Education to provide similar services.

GUIDE FOR SUPERVISORY INTERVIEW

The purposes of supervision are twofold: (1) to help the counselor render as complete a service to the persons who are his responsibility as is possible; and (2) to help the counselor improve his own skills and understanding of human need and the counseling process.

The focus of any individual supervisory session should be on one or more of the following areas: (1) the needs of the person being counseled; (2) the feelings of the counselor; (3) the methods and techniques that are used; (4) the interaction between counselor and counselee; (4) the interaction of the counselee and his environment; and (5) the theological implications of the experience.

The following items are a guide for supervisor and student. The items may or may not be written out. They may or may not all be discussed in one session, and certainly not necessarily in this order.

Background Information: Name _____
Age _____ Sex _____ Marital status _____
Place in the family _____ Siblings _____
Others _____
Is there any test data?

Health Information: What is the general condition of his/her health?

Excellent? _____ Good? _____ Poor? _____

Are there any medical records available?

Any history of chronic or serious illness?

Any physical handicaps or limitations?

Family Background: Were his/her parents happily married? _____ Divorced? _____

Separated? _____

What was the parent's vocation? Husband? _____ Wife? _____

What was the general relationship with parents in childhood?

_____

What is the relationship now? _____

Socio-Economic Position:

What is his/her/their approximate income? _____ Where do they live?

_____ in what part of town? _____

What clubs, organizations do they belong to? _____

_____

According to sociological classification would they be considered: Upper upper

class? _____ Lower upper? _____ Upper middle? _____ Lower middle? _____

Upper lower? _____ Lower lower? _____

What Is the Intellectual Level?

Would he/she be considered: Brilliant? _____ Above average? _____ Normal? _____

Below average? _____ Borderline? _____ Retarded? _____

On what do you base your estimate?

Vocational History and Adjustment:

What is his/her present employment? _____

What previous positions or jobs has he/she held? _____

_____

What are his/her vocational plans and aspirations? _____

_____

What is his/her vocational adjustment? _____

_____

Family Life: What is the nature of his/her home life?

Sex Adjustment: Does he/she understand and accept his/her sexual role?

_____

Any evidences of maladjustment or frustration? _____

_____

Any evidences of deviation? _____

Religious Affiliation:

What is his/her religious affiliation? _____

Has he/she had previous experiences in other religious groups? _____

Is he/she active in his/her church? _____

Does he/she have a good relationship with clergy in general? _____

With his own pastor? _____

Does he/she use religious terms to describe his problem? _____

The Presentation and Nature of the Problem:

What brought him/her/them to the Center? _____

Did they come by self-referral? _____ Referral from a pastor or other professional?

_____ If so, by whom? _____

Does the family know he/she is coming? _____

Did the family pressure him/her to come? _____

What is the problem as he/she stated it?

What do you feel is the real problem?

What are his/her expectations from counseling?

What are the referring agency's expectations?

Does he/she understand the counseling process?

What are his/her immediate needs as he sees them?

What are his/her immediate needs as you see them?

What are his/her long range needs as he sees them?

What are his/her long range needs as you see them?

What non-verbal clues were evident?   Dress?   Posture?

Speech?   Appearance?   Behavior?   Other?

What seemed to be the predominant mood of the person? Confident? _____

Withdrawn? _____ Hostile? _____ Defensive? _____ Anxious? Excited? _____

Resentful? _____ Happy? _____ Other? _____

Did his/her mood change during the interview?

Were there any indications of severe maladjustment? Any physical symptoms? ___

Bizarre behavior? _____ Overreaction? _____ Despondency? _____ Disassociation

with reality? _____ Excessive hostility? _____ Suspicion? _____ Other? _____

Would you consider the problem to be: Situational? _____ Deep-rooted? _____

Long-standing? _____ At the conscious level? _____ Primarily unconscious? _____

Superficial? _____

What do you consider to be this person's or family's major strengths?

Are there latent strengths that could be developed?

Are the environmental factors (home, job, church, etc.) positive?

Are there negative environmental factors?

Does this person have the capacity for insight?

What is his degree of insight? Clear? _____ Confused? _____ Partial? _____

Growing? _____ Could insight be harmful and why? _____

_____

Are there any indications of the need of a referral? If so, what are they?

Would the referral demand the services of a psychiatrist? _____ physician? _____

psychologist? _____ social worker? _____ pastor? _____ other? _____

Methods Used:

What methods did you use? Listening? _____ Reflection? _____ Interpretation? _____

Probing? _____ Confrontation? _____ Advice? _____ Support and reassurance? _____

Why were these methods indicated?

Were they effective? _____ Ineffective? _____ Harmful? _____ Why? _____

_____

Would you anticipate that this situation would respond to continued counseling?

Would it be short-term? _____ Long-term? _____

Were any religious resources used? _____

Prayer? _____ Scripture? _____ Any religious reading or church attendance rec-

ommended? _____

Were any religious ideas discussed?

Were any supplementary resources used? Free writing? _____ Reading? _____

Tasks assigned? _____ Other? _____

If you could repeat the interview, what procedures would you follow that would be

different?

Counselor Reaction: What were your own feelings during the interview and how did

they vary? Comfortable? _____ Tense? _____ Accepting? _____ Angry? _____

Embarrassed? _____ Frustrated? _____ Pleased? _____ Anxious? _____ Impa-

tient? _____

How do you feel toward the person?

How do you think he reacted to you?

What are your plans for the next steps?

APPENDIX 5: MEMO ON STUDY HABITS, A GUIDED INTERVIEW

This section includes the Memo to counselors on Study Habits and a guided-interview blank used with students who are having academic problems. It is part of a packet for study habits that is available to the counselor. The handbook it refers to is the Guidebook Section of the Theological School Check List of Study Skills and Attitudes, by Kemp and Hunt, published by Bethany Press in 1965.

A pastor in a local church could use this material just as well as a counselor in a counseling center.

MEMO TO COUNSELORS OF PASTORAL CARE AND TRAINING CENTER: CONCERNING GUIDANCE IN STUDY HABITS

Young people in high school and college who come to the Center may be having trouble in school. This is seldom the reason for their coming, but, since school occupies so much of their time and energy and has such an important relationship to their general adjustment, any assistance given here may help to establish a good relationship and be of direct practical help academically, and any gains in this area may generalize and increase their self-confidence and their self-concept in other areas as well. It would also be pleasing to their parents.

This is actually more in the field of guidance than in counseling or psychotherapy. Certain suggestions should be kept in mind.

1. The Pastoral Care and Training Center does not attempt to replace or compete with the guidance department of the public school. Whatever is done here should be done in collaboration and cooperation with the school counselor when that is indicated and when it is possible.

2. Grades may merely be a symptom or a result of the young person's problem. One should not get sidetracked with a discussion of grades or study habits which enables both the young person and the counselor to evade the more important issues.

3. Grades, progress in school, the satisfaction and confidence that come from doing well can be very important. The experience of improvement here can influence other areas of experience as is stated in the opening paragraph.

4. Extensive research in educational psychology has produced some definite findings on the principles of learning and the most effective methods of study. The most common of these are summarized in the booklet that is included in this packet. Research has also revealed that very few young people make the best use of their time or talent. Furthermore, such studies show that simple guidance often produces dramatic results.

5. Any effective educational guidance must be based on a person's records (transcripts) and the findings of mental ability, achievement, and interest tests. These can be secured at the school guidance office with the permission of the student involved. If these are inconclusive, individual tests can be administered at the Center or the TCU Testing Office.

6. A guided interview of study skills and attitudes is included in the packet. This enables the student to evaluate his own practices. It also helps the counselor understand the procedures the student is following and gives him some indication of his attitudes toward school and his total preparation.

7. Not infrequently it may lead to a discussion of other matters such as vocational choice, undue pressure of parents, feelings of inadequacy. When this occurs it is usually wise to deal with them through the general counseling sessions, and you may want to delay discussing specific study habits until some of these matters are relieved. If the other problems are not too pressing, they may be done simultaneously.

8. Procedures for administration. The first section of the inventory is for you to fill in as best you can with the information the student provides you. Some facts may need to be secured later at the school guidance office.

The checklist follows the fact sheet. This information is provided entirely by the student. It should be made clear to the student that this is not a test. There are no right or wrong answers. It is an attempt to understand the practices he is now using. He should not depreciate himself, he should not try to look better than he is. The usual procedure is to have him fill in the checklist, either by himself, or audibly, the counselor reading the questions. Together the student and the counselor note the areas that need improvement. These should be specific. In two weeks to a month go over it again. If the student wants a copy as a reminder, remove the fact sheet for your files and give him the checklist.

9. One clear finding of the research on study skills is that one of the most common problems is the inability to schedule and use time. Sometimes this alone will produce surprising improvement. For this reason a schedule blank is included in the packet. The student should be instructed to make an evaluation of his time and go over it with the counselor.

10. The handbook that is included is primarily for the guidance of the counselor. It was prepared originally for seminary students, so some of the items are not applicable to high school or college students. However, the basic principles are as valid for one group as another. The counselor should familiarize himself with this material before attempting any of the procedures above. This could be loaned to the student to give him content, but the supply is limited and they would need to be returned.

STUDY HABITS: GUIDED INTERVIEW
(High School or College)

Name _____ Age _____

School now attending _____

Schools previously attended _____
_____

Grade in school _____

Grade average: High School _____ College _____

Major Subject (if in college) _____

Subjects liked most _____
_____

Subjects liked least _____
_____

(The following information should be filled in when available. Be sure it is accurate. Students are often misinformed about their IQ, etc.)

Mental Ability Tests _____
_____

Achievement Tests _____
_____

Interest Tests _____
_____

Reading Rate _____
_____

Any visual, auditory, speech
or other physical handicaps
that would affect the learning
process.
_____
_____

School Counselor _____
_____

GUIDED INTERVIEW: STUDY SKILLS AND ATTITUDES

Most of the following questions can be answered Always, Occasionally, Usually, or Never. They are designed to lead to a discussion of your total study program. They should be answered the way you now work, not the way you think you "ought" to. Answer frankly, do not be overly critical of yourself, and do not excuse yourself.

		A	U	O	N
1.	Do you enjoy studying?	( )	( )	( )	( )
2.	Do you plan your work for an entire semester?	( )	( )	( )	( )
3.	Do you study a minimum of one hour for each class period?	( )	( )	( )	( )
4.	Do you space your study periods? (For example, if you have three hours to study a subject do you prefer one 3-hour period of continuous study, or do you attempt to arrange it so you have three separate one-hour periods?)	( )	( )	( )	( )
5.	Are your study times long enough to cover sufficient material, but not too long to be fatiguing?	( )	( )	( )	( )
6.	Do you get started immediately in a study period without the need of a warm-up?	( )	( )	( )	( )
7.	Are you able to continue to study when you wish you were doing something else?	( )	( )	( )	( )
8.	Do you give study periods priority over recreation, pleasure, just "goofing off"?	( )	( )	( )	( )
9.	Do you use odd moments (brief periods of time between other activities) for review, extra study, etc.?	( )	( )	( )	( )
10.	Do you have a job, or other demands on your study time that limit the time you can study?	( )	( )	( )	( )
11.	Do you study at a regular time and place?	( )	( )	( )	( )
12.	Do you eliminate all distractions from your time and place of study, such as radio, TV, telephone conversations, etc.?	( )	( )	( )	( )
13.	Do you keep class notes and other materials in an organized file or notebook?	( )	( )	( )	( )
14.	Do you make occasional reviews of your class material?	( )	( )	( )	( )
15.	Do you begin work on an assignment well in advance of the time it is due?	( )	( )	( )	( )
16.	Do you begin preparing for an exam several days before the exam?	( )	( )	( )	( )
17.	Are you thorough in preparation of a paper, theme, or project? Do you recheck for accuracy, spelling, etc.?	( )	( )	( )	( )
18.	Do you seek help when matters are not clear?	( )	( )	( )	( )
19.	Do you tend to postpone work that is difficult?	( )	( )	( )	( )
20.	Do you study beyond the minimum requirements of a course?	( )	( )	( )	( )
21.	Do you turn your work in on time?	( )	( )	( )	( )
22.	Are your papers neat and in good order?	( )	( )	( )	( )

		A	U	O	N
23.	Do you find it easy to participate in classroom discussions?	( )	( )	( )	( )
24.	Do you find it easy to express yourself on paper?	( )	( )	( )	( )
25.	Do you get tense or nervous when taking an exam?	( )	( )	( )	( )
26.	Do you have an interest in all the areas in which you have classes?	( )	( )	( )	( )
27.	Do you work as hard in classes you do not enjoy as in those you do?	( )	( )	( )	( )
28.	Do you see the relationship between your present studies and your future career?	( )	( )	( )	( )
29.	Do you feel there is a relationship between good grades and good study habits?	( )	( )	( )	( )
30.	Do you read rapidly in comparison with others?	( )	( )	( )	( )
31.	Do you read by phrases instead of by words?	( )	( )	( )	( )
32.	Are you able to scan material and get the meaning?	( )	( )	( )	( )
33.	Do you read actively? ask questions of the author? question his findings? his point of view?	( )	( )	( )	( )
34.	Is your general health good?	( )	( )	( )	( )
35.	Do you get sufficient sleep to be alert?	( )	( )	( )	( )
36.	Do you feel you are measuring up to your own ability as a student?	( )	( )	( )	( )
37.	Do you find it easy to concentrate on subject matter without daydreaming?	( )	( )	( )	( )
38.	Do personal concerns keep you from concentrating on your studies?	( )	( )	( )	( )
39.	Does your family encourage you to study?	( )	( )	( )	( )
40.	Does your family put undue pressure on you to get grades?	( )	( )	( )	( )
41.	Are the friends with whom you usually associate good students?	( )	( )	( )	( )

The following statements can be answered "yes" or "no."

1.	Do you plan to go on to college?	( )	( )
2.	Do you plan to go on to graduate school?	( )	( )
3.	Have you made a firm vocational commitment?	( )	( )

Are there other academic matters you wish to discuss? _____

_____

_____

_____

_____

APPENDIX 6: REFERRAL RESOURCES

The following is a list of most of the referral resources that are available to a pastor, with their preferred training and a summary of the services they offer.

Chaplain, Institutional: B.D. or M. Div., and special clinical training in pastoral care.
    Member of staff of state and general hospitals, penal and correctional institutions, homes for older people, schools for retarded, etc.
Chaplain, Military: B.D. or M. Div., and pastoral experience; special training by the military.
Chaplain, University: Regular B.D. or M. Div., often with further graduate work.
    Serves as minister to students on a campus. Usually available for counseling on religious and related problems.
Child Welfare Worker: Social work training
    Specializes in alleviation of child-welfare problems. Attempts to prevent exploitation of minors. Helps physically handicapped children. Finds foster homes and other institutional care. Serves on staff of county and state welfare departments.
Clinical Psychologist: Usually a Ph.D., some only M.A., in psychology.
    Deals with problems of personality, usually specializes in diagnostic tests, such as Rorschach and others. On staff of clinics, universities, or state hospitals; some in private practice.
College Counselor: Usually a Ph.D., sometimes M.A., in educational or clinical psychology.
    Specializes in educational and academic problems, also deals with personality problems. Serves on staff of counseling center at a university, sometimes combines it with teaching.
Employment Worker: No common standard of training.
    Assists people in finding employment. Interviews applicants for jobs, utilizes vocational testing, counseling, etc. Serves on staff of U.S. Employment Service. Some are private agencies.
Family Counselor: Many combinations of training. Usually include psychological, sociological, and social work with emphasis on family life.
    Helps solve problems affecting family, family tension, divorce, care of children, etc. Usually refers psychiatric problems to other specialists. Serves on staff of Family Service Association; some in private practice.
Guidance Worker: Masters in educational psychology preferred minimum.
    Helps with academic and learning problems, specializes in educational and vocational planning. Assists with emotional problems. Staff of large school systems; in smaller schools, also does teaching.
Librarian: Bachelor or Masters degree in library science, some have doctorate.
    Helpful in finding information on any subject. Particularly useful in such areas as family life, occupational life, as supplement to counseling. Staff of city, schools, and universities.

Mission Worker: Religious training, no minimum standard.

Works with transients, lower socio-economic groups. Combines religious and social work approach. Serves on staff of city missions, rescue missions, etc.

Occupational Therapist: A.B., and training in occupational therapy.

Conducts programs for patients in general, mental, and veterans' hospitals to provide them with activity and assist in their rehabilitation. Teaches patients specialized activities, crafts, art, etc.

Parole Officer: Social work training preferred. Many do not have it.

Works with delinquents and criminals who are on parole from corrective institutions, attempts help with rehabilitation.

Pastoral Counselor as a specialist: B.D. or M. Div., and special training in pastoral care.

some in private practice.

Probation Officer: Social work training preferred. Many do not have it.

Responsible for delinquents who are on probation; takes case histories, counsels, works with courts.

Psychiatric Social Worker: M.S.W., minimum.

Does casework with persons suffering from nervous or emotional problems. Usually on staff of hospital or institution.

Psychiatrist: M.D. and psychiatric training.

Specializes in treatment of nervous and emotional diseases. Serves on staff of hospitals, child guidance clinics, or in private practice.

Psychoanalyst: M.D., plus psychiatric training plus analytic training, including a lengthy analysis. Specializes in treatment of nervous and emotional disease by Freudian or neo-Freudian analysis. Treatment is usually long-term.

Psychometrist: M.A. or Ph.D., in Psychology and Mental Measurements.

Specializes in mental testing. Usually on staff of university counseling service, or clinic. Often combines with teaching.

Public Health Nurse: Nurse's Training.

Available for service in public health department, also in homes, with elderly, maternity care, etc. Staff of department of public health.

Red Cross Worker: Social work training preferred, although not all have it.

Provides communication for servicemen in need of leave, etc. Services in disaster areas. Home service department does some casework counseling.

Rehabilitation Office: Counsels adults with problems of vocational choice and training.

Salvation Army Worker: Special training by Salvation Army.

Carries on variety of services, work with transients, unwed mothers, find employment, religious welfare work, etc. Salvation Army office created almost everywhere.

School Psychologist: M.A., sometimes Ph.D., in educational psychology.

Specializes in testing, counseling or academic problems, and vocational choice, also mild emotional problems. Staff of larger school systems.

Social Worker: Masters degree in social work.

Covers many fields; works to alleviate and prevent social problems by providing counseling, monetary grants, vocational and avocational opportunities. Especially well acquainted with community resources. Serves on staff of private and religious agencies, government, state, federal, and county.

Speech Therapist: A.B. or equivalent, and graduate training in speech therapy.

Assists people with problems of speech, stuttering, poor articulation, etc. On staff of educational institutions.

Travelers Aid Worker: Social work training preferred, not a requirement.

Assists in solving problems due to travel, helps children traveling alone, helps people who are lost. Aids travelers in need of financial assistance. Helps transients find their destination.

Visiting Teacher: A.B., teaching experience, plus social work training.

Assists children who find difficulty in adapting to school life. Counsels with children who need individual help, and with their parents. Arranges for medical, psychiatric, and other services when indicated.

Vocational Counselor: A.B. and Masters or Doctoral degree in vocational counseling.

Assists students and others in selecting and training for a career. Does vocational testing, vocational counseling. Specializes in occupational information. Serves on staff of schools and colleges; some in private practice.

Welfare Worker: Social work training.

Administers welfare funds, counsels and assists families on relief. Staff of city and state welfare departments.

YMCA, YWCA: Training varies. Certification indicates a minimum of 30 graduate hours, including counseling, religion, and group work. On staff of YMCA and YWCA.

APPENDIX 7: THE ATTITUDES OF THE PASTORAL COUNSELOR

Fred McKinney, in his book Counseling for Personal Adjustment, includes a chapter on "The Counseling Relationship." He includes a list of adjectives which characterize typical counseling relationships. These terms apply to the pastoral relationship as well. Many, though not all, of the following terms are taken from McKinney's list. Consider your most recent pastoral counseling experiences and underline those adjectives that would characterize your relationships with counselees.

formal	businesslike	passive
warm	condescending	objective
dependent	coercive	mechanical
artificial	sincere	professional
embarrassed	accepting	clumsy
cool	professional	pious
open	pastoral	strained
confident	impersonal	authoritative
awkward	permissive	anxious
tense	calm	relaxed
co-working	active	hurried
sympathetic	understanding	dominative
secure	friendly	
submissive	probing	

APPENDIX 8: CHECKLIST OF COUNSELING PRINCIPLES AND PROCEDURES

This checklist is designed to provide a means whereby you can check yourself as to how you are applying the principles and techniques of counseling and psychotherapy. There are no right or wrong answers for any specific case. This will help you understand how you feel about principles and techniques. With your most recent counseling experiences in mind check the items in the right-hand columns and discuss them with a well-trained pastor, psychologist, psychiatrist, or supervisor in a counseling center. Recheck yourself at regular intervals.

The four columns are to be checked as follows: (A) if your practice is always, (U) if it is something you usually do, (O) if it is your practice to follow this procedure occasionally, and (N) if it is never.

	(A)	(U)	(O)	(N)
1. Do you see each person as a person of unconditional worth?	( )	( )	( )	( )
2. Do you give human need the first priority over all other matters?	( )	( )	( )	( )
3. Do you have attitudes of genuine acceptance toward people who do not agree with your theological position?	( )	( )	( )	( )
4. Do you have attitudes of genuine acceptance toward people whose behavior you cannot accept?	( )	( )	( )	( )
5. Are you able to understand how another person feels?	( )	( )	( )	( )
6. Do you treat a counselee as an equal?	( )	( )	( )	( )
7. Are you able to maintain concentration in a person and his problems?	( )	( )	( )	( )
8. Do you ask meaningless questions?	( )	( )	( )	( )
9. Do you ask questions that the counselee cannot answer?	( )	( )	( )	( )
10. Do you request clarification when you do not understand?	( )	( )	( )	( )
11. Do you permit the counselee to tell his own story in his own way?	( )	( )	( )	( )
12. Are you careful not to arouse too much anxiety at any one time?	( )	( )	( )	( )
13. Do you utilize supplementary resources such as the reading of books or pamphlets?	( )	( )	( )	( )
14. Do you avoid the tendency to pry or probe for information out of curiosity?	( )	( )	( )	( )
15. Do you listen more than you talk?	( )	( )	( )	( )

		(A)	(U)	(O)	(N)
16.	Do you check over records of previous interviews before each interview?	( )	( )	( )	( )
17.	Do you define your role so the counselee understands the nature and purposes of the counseling process?	( )	( )	( )	( )
18.	Do you use occasional feedback questions to be sure real communication is taking place?	( )	( )	( )	( )
19.	Do you see maladjustment or misbehavior as a symptom of a need?	( )	( )	( )	( )
20.	Do you keep in mind that all behavior is purposive and therefore must be seen as striving to meet unfulfilled needs?	( )	( )	( )	( )
21.	Do you act on the concept that people have within themselves the capacity to change, mature, improve, grow?	( )	( )	( )	( )
22.	Do you act on the concept that people are capable of handling their own lives, of making their own decisions?	( )	( )	( )	( )
23.	Do you recognize that all people have differences of ability, background, and interest and must be dealt with accordingly?	( )	( )	( )	( )
24.	Are you careful to check whether you are using words in the same way as the counselee?	( )	( )	( )	( )
25.	Do you use language the counselee can understand?	( )	( )	( )	( )
26.	Do you note all nonverbal clues to behavior?	( )	( )	( )	( )
27.	Do you have any theoretical biases that influence your evaluation of a situation.	( )	( )	( )	( )
28.	Do you permit the counselee to make his own decisions?	( )	( )	( )	( )
29.	Do you reenforce every move toward health?	( )	( )	( )	( )
30.	Are you alert to evidences of transference?	( )	( )	( )	( )
31.	Are you alert to evidences of countertransference?	( )	( )	( )	( )
32.	Do you look for strengths in each situation?	( )	( )	( )	( )
33.	Do you use personal experiences as illustrations?	( )	( )	( )	( )
34.	Do you seek help from a supervisor or a specialist, or an agency if you feel they are more qualified to deal with a situation than you are?	( )	( )	( )	( )
35.	Do you insist that all physical symptoms described by a counselee be checked by a doctor?	( )	( )	( )	( )
36.	Are you willing to refer a person whom you feel you cannot help?	( )	( )	( )	( )

	(A)	(U)	(O)	(N)
37. Do you follow up on all referrals?	( )	( )	( )	( )
38. Do you believe God is really concerned about these persons?	( )	( )	( )	( )
39. Do you utilize religious resources, such as prayer and scripture?	( )	( )	( )	( )
40. Do you discuss religious ideas, or religious interpretations of life problems with counselees?	( )	( )	( )	( )
41. Are you honest in all your dealings with a counselee?	( )	( )	( )	( )
42. Do you keep all information strictly confidential?	( )	( )	( )	( )
43. Do you promise success in counseling?	( )	( )	( )	( )
44. Are you careful that any information you give is accurate and up-to-date?	( )	( )	( )	( )
45. Are you prompt and dependable in meeting appointments?	( )	( )	( )	( )
46. If you tape-record an interview, do you secure the counselee's permission?	( )	( )	( )	( )
47. Do you have faith in the methods that you use?	( )	( )	( )	( )
48. Are you willing to struggle with a person for a long period of time, even if little manifest progress seems to result?	( )	( )	( )	( )
49. Do you feel successful in every counseling situation?	( )	( )	( )	( )
50. Do you have insight into your own needs and limitations?	( )	( )	( )	( )
51. Do you accept yourself as you are?	( )	( )	( )	( )
52. Are you able to remain objective when discussing emotional material?	( )	( )	( )	( )
53. Are you able to shut out distractions, other responsibilities, and interests when counseling?	( )	( )	( )	( )
54. When counseling, do you have the feeling that this is the most important thing you could be doing?	( )	( )	( )	( )
55. Do you attempt to impress a counselee with your knowledge or authority?	( )	( )	( )	( )
56. Do you become impatient or hostile to some counselees?	( )	( )	( )	( )
57. Do you tend to sermonize?	( )	( )	( )	( )
58. Do you tend to argue, exhort, or coerce?	( )	( )	( )	( )
59. Are you able to accept setbacks without becoming disturbed or offended?	( )	( )	( )	( )
60. Do you insist that persons' goals for themselves agree with your goals for them?	( )	( )	( )	( )

		(A)	(U)	(O)	(N)
61.	Are you genuinely interested in persons?	( )	( )	( )	( )
62.	Are you able to be nonpunitive in the presence of material that is offensive or morally disgusting?	( )	( )	( )	( )
63.	Do you ever control or manipulate your counselees?	( )	( )	( )	( )
64.	Are you uncomfortable counseling people older than you are?	( )	( )	( )	( )
65.	Are you comfortable counseling people younger than you are?	( )	( )	( )	( )
66.	Do you feel uncomfortable when a counselee manifests extreme hostility?	( )	( )	( )	( )
67.	Do you feel uncomfortable if a counselee is discussing sexual matters?	( )	( )	( )	( )
68.	Are you comfortable counseling someone from a religious background very different from your own?	( )	( )	( )	( )
69.	Do you feel uncomfortable if a counselee attacks your religious position?	( )	( )	( )	( )
70.	Do you feel uncomfortable when a counselee wants to argue?	( )	( )	( )	( )
71.	Are you comfortable counseling members of another race?	( )	( )	( )	( )
72.	Do you feel comfortable and relaxed in the interview?	( )	( )	( )	( )
73.	When counseling, do you wear clothes appropriate for the occasion?	( )	( )	( )	( )
74.	Are you able to give the impression of being unhurried?	( )	( )	( )	( )
75.	Do you inform the counselee of the time limits within which you are operating?	( )	( )	( )	( )
76.	Do you feel uncomfortable during long pauses?	( )	( )	( )	( )
77.	Do you schedule sufficient time for each interview?	( )	( )	( )	( )
78.	Are your dress, the desk, or other matters in the room free from distraction?	( )	( )	( )	( )
79.	Do you make a record of the interview immediately following the session?	( )	( )	( )	( )
80.	If you take notes during an interview, do you explain why?	( )	( )	( )	( )

APPENDIX 9 : ANNOTATED BIBLIOGRAPHY

The literature on pastoral psychology, pastoral counseling, and pastoral care has had remarkable growth in the last few decades. The student of pastoral care must be familiar not only with this field of writing, but also with the basic publications in the related fields of psychology, psychiatry, mental hygiene, and family counseling. He may benefit too by having a knowledge of what is happening in such fields as geriatrics, alcoholism, vocational counseling, and other special areas. All these have a bearing on pastoral care.

The following bibliography is arranged by areas of study. Some of the books listed deal with general background material, some with specific problems. Most have been prepared for pastors, although books from the secular disciplines are also included. The books are arranged within an area, not according to their importance, but in simple alphabetical order.

No attempt has been made to include every title --that would be impossible, since new studies are appearing almost daily. The serious student of pastoral care will preserve a regular time to read and keep abreast of the growing knowledge in how people can be served.

An outline and some self-scoring examinations are provided in my workbook Learning About Pastoral Care, which was published by Abingdon in 1970. You can check the effectiveness of your reading by administering these exams to yourself.

General Books: Pastoral Counseling and Pastoral Care

There are several good overall discussions of the pastoral tasks. Some cover the entire range of pastoral responsibilities, some give primary emphasis to counseling as such. Some of the better books are:

Brister, C. W. Pastoral Care in the Church. New York: Harper & Row, 1964.

Clinebell, Howard W. Basic Types of Pastoral Counseling. Nashville: Abingdon, 1966.

Hiltner, Seward. Pastoral Counseling. Apex Book; Nashville: Abingdon, (1949) 1969.

_____. The Christian Shepherd. Nashville: Abingdon, 1959.

Johnson, Paul E. The Psychology of Pastoral Care. Apex Book; Nashville: Abingdon, (1953) 1964.

Oates, Wayne. Protestant Pastoral Counseling. Philadelphia: Westminster, 1962.

——. The Christian Pastor. Rev. ed. Philadelphia: Westminster, 1964.

Wise, Carroll. Pastoral Counseling: Its Theory and Practice. New York: Harpers, 1951.

Historical Interpretation of Pastoral Care

HISTORICAL STUDIES

Clebsch, W. A. and Jaekle, E. R. Pastoral Care in Historical Perspective. Englewood Cliffs, N. J.: Prentice-Hall, 1964.

Kemp, Charles F. Physicians of the Soul. New York: Macmillan, 1947.

McNeill, John T. A History of the Cure of Souls. New York: Harpers, 1951.

McNeill, John T., and Gamer, Helena M. Medieval Handbooks of Penance. New York: Octagon Books, (1938) 1965.

Nebe, August. Luther as Spiritual Adviser. Lutheran Publication Society, 1894.

Niebuhr, H. Richard, and Williams, Daniel. The Ministry in Historial Perspective. New York: Harper & Row, 1956.

Tappert, Theodore, ed. Luther: Letters of Spiritual Counsel. Philadelphia: Westminster, 1955.

BIOGRAPHY AND AUTOBIOGRAPHY

The biography or autobiography of any outstanding pastor would be useful for this purpose. The following deal with effective pastors who had distinguished careers:

Allen, A. V. G. Life of Phillips Brooks. New York: Dutton, 1907.

Baxter, Richard. Autobiography. Everyman's Library, 1931.

Beard, Augustus F. Life of John Frederic Oberlin. Philadelphia: Pilgrim Press, 1909.

Cheney, Margaret. Life and Letters of Horace Bushnell. New York: Scribner's, 1909.

Fosdick, Harry Emerson. The Living of These Days. New York: Harper & Row, 1956.

Gladden, Washington. Recollections. New York: Houghton Mifflin, 1909.

Kemp, Charles F. A Pastoral Triumph (The Pastoral Ministry of Richard Baxter). New York: Macmillan, 1947.

Nicoll, W. Robertson. Life of John Watson (Ian MacLaren). London: Hodder & Stoughton, 1908.

Sharpe, Doris. Walter Rauschenbusch. New York: Macmillan, 1942.

Smith, George Adam. Life of Henry Drummond. New York: Doubleday and McClure, 1898.

CLASSICS OF PASTORAL CARE

Some books that have been very influential in the pastoral ministry and can rightfully be called classics are:

Baxter, Richard. The Reformed Pastor. Naperville, Ill.: Allenson, 1956.

Gladden, Washington. The Christian Pastor. New York: Scribner's, (1898) 1904.

Herbert, George. The Country Parson. London: SCM, 1956.

Jefferson, Charles. The Minister as Shepherd. New York: Crowell, 1912.

MacLaren, Ian. The Cure of Souls. New York: Dodd, Mead, 1896.

Worcester, McComb, and Coriat. Religion and Medicine. London: Moffatt, Yard, 1908.

General Psychology

Next to taking course work, the best way of attaining a knowledge of psychology is to do extensive reading in the field. A good contemporary introduction to psychology will bring one up-to-date and reenforce the knowledge one already has. Working through a programmed learning course in psychology is perhaps the most effective form of self-study--far more effective than just reading--and is the best stewardship of time.

Some texts used in introductory courses in psychology have workbooks accompanying them. Portions of these are programmed, and working through one or more would be the equivalent of taking a regular course in psychology.

Hilgard, Ernest R. Introduction to Psychology. 3rd ed. New York: Harcourt, Brace and World, 1962. Student Guide with Programmed Units by Teevan and Jandron available.

Whittaker, James O. An Introduction to Psychology and Student's Workbook to Accompany an Introduction to Psychology. 2nd ed. Philadelphia: Saunders, 1965.

Some courses have been programmed to be worked through on teaching machines. Others have been programmed in book form and can be done at home, such as the following:

Holland, James, and Skinner, B. F. The Analysis of Behavior. New York: McGraw-Hill, 1961.

Malpass, Leslie F. et al. Human Behavior: A Program of Self-Instruction. New York: McGraw-Hill, 1961.

Fernald, L. Dodge, Jr., and Fernald, Peter. Overview of General Psychology: A Basic Program. New York: Houghton Mifflin, 1966.

HISTORY OF PSYCHOLOGY, MEDICAL PSYCHOLOGY, AND PSYCHOTHERAPY

Bloomburg, Walter. Man Above Humanity. Philadelphia: Lippincott, 1959.

Boring, Edwin. A History of Experimental Psychology. New York: Appleton-Century-Crofts, 1950.

Murphy, Gardner. Historical Introduction to Modern Psychology. Rev. ed. New York: Harcourt, Brace, 1949.

Roback, Abraham A. History of American Psychology. New York: Macmillan paperback, (1952)1964.

Walker, Nigel. A Short History of Psychotherapy. New York: Norton, 1941.

Zilboorg, Gregory, and Henry, George W. A History of Medical Psychology. New York: Norton, 1941.

PERSONALITY THEORY

Allport, Gordon W. Pattern and Growth in Personality. New York; Holt, Rinehart and Winston, 1961.

Bischof, Ledford. Interpreting Personality Theories. 3rd ed. New York: Harper & Row, (1964) 1970.

Dreger, Ralph M. Fundamentals of Personality. New York: Lippincott, 1962.

Hall, Calvin, and Lindzey, Gardner. Theories of Personality. 2nd ed. New York: John Wiley, (1957) 1970.

Lazarus, Richard. Personality and Adjustment. New York: Prentice-Hall, 1963.

Lindzey, Gardner, and Hall, Calvin. Readings in Theories of Personality. New York: John Wiley, 1963.

Wolman, Benjamin. Contemporary Theories and Systems in Psychology. New York: Harper & Row, 1960.

ABNORMAL PSYCHOLOGY AND MENTAL HYGIENE

Cameron, Norman. Personality Development and Psychopathology. New York: Houghton Mifflin, 1963.

Coleman, James C. Abnormal Psychology and Modern Life. 3rd ed. Glenview, Ill.: Scott, Foresman, 1964.

Maslow, Abraham H., and Mittlemann, Bela. Principles of Abnormal Psychology. New York: Harpers, 1941.

Pronko, Nicholas. Textbook of Abnormal Psychology. Baltimore: Williams and Wilkins, 1963.

White, Robert W. The Abnormal Personality. 3rd ed. New York: Ronald Press, 1964.

SOCIAL PSYCHOLOGY

Cartwright, Dorwin, and Zander, Alvin, eds. Group Dynamics: Research and Theory. 3rd ed. New York: Harper & Row, (1960) 1968.

Klineberg, Otto. Social Psychology. New York: Holt, Rinehart and Winston, 1954.

Lewin, Kurt et al. Readings in Social Psychology. New York: Holt, Rinehart and Winston, 1952.

Lindzey, Gardner. Handbook of Social Psychology. 5 vols. 2nd ed. Reading, Mass.: Addison-Wesley, 1968.

Sherif, Muzafer, and Sherif, Carolyn. Social Psychology. 3rd ed. Harper College Books; New York: Harper & Row, (1956) 1969.

FOR UNDERSTANDING TERMINOLOGY

English, Horace B., and English, Ava C. A Comprehensive Dictionary of Psychological and Psychoanalytical Terms: A Guide to Usage. New York: David McKay, 1958.

Schools of Counseling

FOR FURTHER STUDY

Several volumes have made an attempt to summarize the various schools of counseling and psychotherapy. Some have done so very well, such as:

Ford, Donald H., and Urban, Hugh B. Systems of Psychotherapy. New York: John Wiley, 1963.

Stein, Morris J., ed. Contemporary Psychotherapies. New York: Free Press, 1961.

Patterson, Cecil H. Theories of Counseling and Psychotherapy. New York: Harper and Row, 1966.

Each school has an extensive list of original sources from the writings of Freud to the more recent publications of the Learning Theorists and Existentialists. Most of the books such as those listed above have bibliographies of the separate schools.

PSYCHOANALYSIS

Blum, Gerald S. Psychoanalytic Theories of Personality. New York: McGraw-Hill, 1953.

Feruchel, O. The Psychoanalytic Theory of the Neurosis. New York: Norton, 1945.

Freud, Sigmund. A General Introduction to Psychoanalysis. Rev. ed. Clarion Book; New York: Simon & Shuster, (1920) 1969.

_____. Interpretation of Dreams. Tr. James J. Strachey. New York: Basic Books, (1953) 1955.

_____. An Outline of Psychoanalysis. Ed. James J. Strachey. New York: Norton, 1970.

_____. Psychopathology of Everyday Life. Tr. Alan Tyson. New York: Norton, (1959) 1966.

_____. The Standard Edition of the Complete Works of Freud. London: Hogarth, 1953.

Hall, C. S. A Primer of Freudian Psychology. New York: World, 1954.

Jones, Ernest. The Life and Work of Sigmund Freud. 3 vols. New York: Basic Books, 1961.

INDIVIDUAL PSYCHOLOGY

Adler, Alfred. The Practice and Theory of Individual Psychology. Tr. P. Radin. New York: Humanities Press, (1927) 1951.

_____. Understanding Human Nature. Tr. W. B. Wolfe. Premier Book; New York: Fawcett World, (1927) 1968.

_____. What Life Should Mean to You. Ed. Alan Porter. Capricorn Book; New York: G. P. Putnam, (1931) 1959.

Adler, Kurt, and Deutsch, Donica. Essays in Individual Psychology. New York: Grove Press, 1959.

Ansbacher, Heinz L., and Ansbacher, Rowena R. The Individual Psychology of Alfred Adler. New York: Basic Books, 1956.

Dreikurs, Rowena. Fundamentals of Adlerian Psychology. New York: Greenberg, 1950.

Way, Lewis. Adler's Place in Psychology. New York: Collier, 1962.

JUNG: ANALYTIC PSYCHOLOGY

Fordham, Frieda. An Introduction to Jung's Psychology. Baltimore: Penguin Books, 1953.

Jacobi, J. The Psychology of Jung. New Haven: Yale University Press, 1951.

Jung, Carl C. Modern Man in Search of a Soul. New York: Harcourt, Brace, 1961.

————. Collected Papers on Analytical Psychology.

————. Collected Works. 18 vols. Bollingen Series. Ed. Herbert Read et al. Tr. R.F.C. Hull. Princeton, N.J.: Princeton University, 1953.

————. Psychology of the Unconscious. London: Moffatt, Yard, 1916.

————. Psychology and Religion. London: Oxford University Press, 1938.

CLINICAL COUNSELING

Bordin, E. S. Psychological Counseling. New York: Appleton-Century-Crofts, 1955.

Hahn, Milton, and MacLean, Malcolm. General Clinical Counseling. New York: McGraw-Hill, 1950.

CLIENT-CENTERED THERAPY

Porter, E. An Introduction to Therapeutic Counseling. Boston: Houghton Mifflin, 1942.

Rogers, Carl. Client-Centered Therapy. Boston: Houghton Mifflin, 1951.

————. Counseling and Psychotherapy. Boston: Houghton Mifflin, 1942.

————. On Becoming a Person. Boston: Houghton Mifflin, 1961.

Rogers, Carl, and Dymond, R. Psychotherapy and Personality Change. Chicago: University of Chicago Press, 1954.

Snyder, William U. Case Studies in Client-Centered Therapy. Boston: Houghton Mifflin.

NEO-FREUDIANISM: NEW THEORIES IN PSYCHOANALYSIS

Erikson, Erik H. Childhood and Society. Rev. ed. New York: Norton, (1950) 1964.

_____. Identity and the Life Cycle. Psychological Issues. New York: International Universities Press, 1959.

_____. The Young Man Luther. New York: Norton, 1958.

Fromm, Erich. The Art of Loving. New York: Harper & Row, (1950) 1956.

_____. Escape from Freedom. New York: Avon Books, (1941) 1969.

_____. Man for Himself. New York: Premier Book; Fawcett World, (1947) 1968.

_____. Psychoanalysis and Religion. New York: Bantam Book, (1950) 1970.

Glen, J. Stanley. Erich Fromm, a Protestant Critique. Philadelphia: Westminster, 1966.

Horney, Karen, Neurosis and Human Growth. New York: Norton Paperback, (1950) 1970.

_____. The Neurotic Personality of Our Time. New York: Norton, 1937.

_____. New Ways in Psychoanalysis. New York: Norton, 1939.

_____. Our Inner Conflicts. New York: Norton, 1945.

_____. Self-Analysis. New York: Norton, 1942.

Menninger, Karl. Theory of Psychoanalytic Technique. New York: Basic Books, 1959.

_____. The Vital Balance. New York: Viking, 1963.

Rank, Otto. Beyond Psychology. New York: Dover Paperback, (1941) 1959.

_____. Psychology and the Soul. Paperback; New York: A. S. Barnes, 1961.

_____. Trauma of Birth. New York: Basic Books, (1952) 1953.

_____. Will Therapy and Truth and Reality. New York: Knopf, 1945.

Sullivan, Harry Stack. Conceptions of Modern Psychiatry. New York: Norton, (1953) 1968.

————. The Interpersonal Theory of Psychiatry. New York: Norton (1953) 1968.

————. The Psychiatric Interview. New York: Norton, 1954.

EXISTENTIAL PSYCHOLOGY

May, Rollo, ed. Existence: A New Dimension in Psychiatry and Psychology. Clarion Book; New York: Simon & Schuster, (1958) 1967.

————. Existential Psychology, 2nd Ed. New York: Random House, 1961.

Reutenbeck, Hendrik, ed. Psychoanalysis and Existential Philosophy. New York: Dutton, 1962.

Sonnemann, Ulrich. Existence and Therapy. New York: Grune and Stratton, 1954.

LOGOTHERAPY

Bugental, J. F. T. The Search for Authenticity: An Existentialist-Analytic Approach to Psychotherapy. New York: Holt, Rinehart and Winston, 1965.

Frankl, Viktor. The Doctor and the Soul. Rev. ed. New York: Alfred A. Knopf, (1957) 1965.

————. Man's Search for Meaning: An Introduction to Logotherapy. Rev. ed. New York: Beacon, (1959) 1963.

Leslie, Robert. Jesus and Logotherapy. Apex Books; Nashville: Abingdon, (1965) 1968.

Tweedie, Donald F. Logotherapy and the Christian Faith. Baker, 1961.

Ungersma, A. J. The Search for Meaning. Paperback; Philadelphia: Westminster, (1961) 1968.

INTEGRITY THERAPY

Drakeford, John. Integrity Therapy, a New Direction in Psychotherapy. Nashville: Broadman, (1965) 1967.

Mowrer, O. Hobart. The Crisis in Psychiatry and Religion. New York: Van Nostrand, 1961.

_____. Learning Theory and Behavior. New York: John Wiley, 1960.

_____. The New Group Therapy. New York: Van Nostrand, 1964.

REALITY THERAPY

Glasser, William. Reality Therapy, a New Approach to Psychiatry. New York: Harper & Row, 1965.

LEARNING THEORY AND BEHAVIOR MODIFICATION

Dollard and Miller. Personality and Psychotherapy. New York: McGraw-Hill, 1950.

Eysench, H. J. Behaviour Therapy and the Neuroses. Elmsford, N.Y.: Pergamon Press, 1962.

Krasner, L. and Ullmann, L. P. Research in Behavior Modification. New York: Holt, Rinehart & Winston, 1966.

Krumboltz, John D., ed. Revolution in Counseling. Boston: Houghton Mifflin, 1966.

Krumboltz, John, and Thoresen, Carl E. Behavioral Counseling. New York: Holt, Rinehart and Winston, 1969.

London, Perry. The Modes and Morals of Psychotherapy. 2nd ed. New York: Holt, Rinehart and Winston, (1964) 1970.

Salter, Andrew. Conditional Reflex Therapy. Capricorn Book; New York: G. P. Putnam's Sons, (1949) 1961.

Ullmann, L. P. and Krasner, L. Case Studies in Behavior Modification. New York: Holt, Rinehart and Winston, 1965.

Wolpe, J. Psychotherapy by Reciprocal Inhibition. Stanford, Calif.: Stanford University Press, 1958.

Yates, Aubrey. Behavior Therapy. New York: John Wiley & Sons, 1969.

GESTALT THERAPY

Fagan, Joen, and Shepherd, Irma Lee. Gestalt Therapy Now. Palo Alto, Calif. Science and Behavior Books, 1970.

Perls, Frederick, Hefferline, Ralph, and Goodman, Paul. Gestalt Therapy. New York: Julian Press, 1969.

ECLECTIC THEORY

McKinney, Fred. Counseling for Personal Adjustment in Schools and Colleges. Boston: Houghton Mifflin, 1958.

Thorne, Frederick. Principles of Personality Counseling. Brandon, Vt.: Journal of Clinical Psychology, 1950.

The Interview

Books on the pastoral interview are listed in the section Pastoral Counseling Techniques. Other disciplines also use the interview and some of their publications are helpful for the pastor.

Bingham, Walter, and Moore, Bruce. How to Interview. 4th ed. New York: Harper & Row, 1959.

Freeman, Harrop A. Legal Interviewing and Counseling. St. Paul, Minn.: West, 1964.

Sullivan, Harry S. The Psychiatric Interview. New York: Norton, 1954.

Listening

Most books mentioned in other sections discuss the value of listening. A few have been written that deal with it throughout the entire volume such as:

Barbara, Dominick A. The Art of Listening. Springfield, Ill.: Charles C. Thomas, 1958.

Faber, Heije, and Van der Schoot, E. The Art of Pastoral Conversation. Nashville: Abingdon, 1965.

Steere, Douglas V. On Listening to Another. New York: Harper & Row, (1955) 1964.

A brief bibliography for those wanting further information about the principles of psychological testing.

Anastasi, Anne. Psychological Testing. 3rd ed. New York: Macmillan, (1954) 1968.

Cronbach, Lee. Essentials of Psychological Testing. 3rd ed. New York: Harper & Row, (1949) 1970.

Freeman, Frank. Theory and Practice of Psychological Testing. 3rd ed. New York: Holt, Rinehart and Winston, (1950) 1963.

Goldman, Leo. Using Tests in Counseling. New York: Appleton-Century-Crofts, 1961.

Goodenough, Florence L. Mental Testing. Chicago: Johnson, (1950) 1969.

Referral

Kemp, Charles F. The Pastor and Community Resources. St..Louis: Bethany Press, 1960.

Oates, Wayne. Where to Go for Help. Philadelphia: Westminster, 1967.

Oglesby, William. Referral in Pastoral Counseling. Philadelphia: Fortress, 1969.

Marriage and Family

FAMILY LIFE IN CONTEMPORARY SOCIETY

Crook, Roger H. The Changing American Family. St. Louis: Bethany Press, 1960.

Denton, Wallace. What's Happening to Our Families? Philadelphia: Westminster, 1963.

MARRIAGE AND FAMILY LIFE (GENERAL)

Ackerman, Nathan W. The Psychodynamics of Family Life. New York: Basic Books, 1958.

Burke, Louis H. With This Ring. New York: McGraw-Hill, 1958.

Carrington, W. L. The Healing of Marriage. New York: Channel Press, 1961.

Duvall, Evelyn M., and Hill, Reuben L. Being Married. Lexington, Mass.: Heath, 1960.

McGinnis, Tom. Your First Year of Marriage. New York: Doubleday, 1967.

Mudd, Emily. Man and Wife. New York: Norton, 1957.

Peterson, James. Toward a Successful Marriage. New York: Scribner's, 1960.

Popenoe, Paul. Marriage Is What You Make It. New York: Macmillan, 1950.

Womble, Dale. Foundations for Marriage and Family Relations. New York: Macmillan, 1966.

Wood, Leland F. How Love Grows in Marriage. New York: Macmillan, 1950.

GENERAL MARRIAGE COUNSELING

Johnson, Dean. Marriage Counseling: Theory and Practice. Englewood Cliffs, N. J.: Prentice-Hall, 1961.

Mudd, Emily. The Practice of Marriage Counseling. New York: Association Press, 1951.

Peterson, James, ed. Marriage & Family Counseling. New York: Association Press, 1968.

Satir, Virginia. Conjoint Family Therapy: A Guide to Theory and Technique. Rev. ed. Palo Alto, Calif.: Science & Behavior Books, (1964) 1967.

Skidmore, Rex Austin, et al. Marriage Consulting. New York: Harpers, 1956.

PREMARITAL PASTORAL COUNSELING

Morris, James K. Premarital Counseling: A Manual for Ministers. Englewood Cliffs, N. J.: Prentice-Hall, 1960.

Oates, Wayne E. Premarital Pastoral Care and Counseling. Nashville: Broadman, 1958.

Rutledge, Aaron L. Premarital Counseling. Cambridge, Mass.: Schenkman, 1966.

Westberg, Granger. Premarital Counseling: A Manual for Ministers. New York: National Council of Churches, 1958.

PASTORAL COUNSELING ON FAMILY LIFE

Hulme, William E. Pastoral Care of Families: Its Theology and Practice. Nashville: Abingdon, 1962.

Morris, J. Kenneth. Marriage Counseling: a Manual for Ministers. Englewood Cliffs, N. J.: Prentice-Hall, 1965.

Stewart, Charles W. The Minister as Marriage Counselor. Rev. ed. Nashville: Abingdon, (1961) 1971.

Wynn, John C. Pastoral Ministry to Families. Philadelphia: Westminster, 1957.

AN INTERPRETATION OF SEX

Bailey, Derrick S. Common Sense About Sexual Ethics. New York: Macmillan, 1962.

————. Sexual Relations in Christian Thought. New York: Harper & Row, 1959.

Baruch, Dorothy, and Miller, Hyman. Sex in Marriage. New York: Harper & Row, 1962.

Cole, William G. Sex and Love in the Bible. New York: Association Press, 1959.

————. Sex in Christianity and Psychoanalysis. New York: Oxford University Press, 1955.

Duvall, Evelyn M., and Duvall, S. M. Sex Ways in Fact and Faith. New York: Association Press, 1961.

Eckert, Ralph G. Sex Attitudes in the Home. New York: Association Press, 1956.

Lewin, S. A. and Gilmore, John. Sex Without Fear. New York: Medical Research Press, 1951.

Piper, Otto A. The Biblical View of Sex and Marriage. New York: Scribner's, 1960.

Thielicke, Helmut. The Ethics of Sex. New York: Harper & Row, 1964.

RELIGION, THE HOME, AND FAMILY

Bailey, Derrick S. The Mystery of Love and Marriage. New York: Harper & Row, 1952.

Bainton, Roland H. What Christianity Says About Sex, Love and Marriage. New York: Association Press, 1957.

Bossard, James H. One Marriage, Two Faiths. New York: Ronald Press, 1957.

Bowman, Henry A. A Christian Interpretation of Marriage. Philadelphia: Westminster, 1959.

Emerson, James G. Divorce, the Church and Remarriage. Philadelphia: Westminster, 1961.

Fairchild, Roy, and Wynn, John. Families in the Church. New York: Association Press, 1961.

Gordon, Albert I. Intermarriage: Interfaith, Interracial, Interethnic. Boston: Beacon Press, 1964.

Hulme, William. Building a Christian Marriage. Englewood Cliffs, N.J.: Prentice-Hall, 1965.

Mace, David R. Whom God Hath Joined. Philadelphia: Westminster, 1953.

Wood, Leland F. Harmony in Marriage. Manhasset, N.Y.: Round Table Press, 1939.

FOR OBSERVATION AND FURTHER INFORMATION:

Visit the Family Service Association and discuss the type of problems they deal with and how a minister can work cooperatively with them.

Vocational Guidance and Adjustment

THE PASTOR AND VOCATIONAL COUNSELING

Kemp, Charles F. The Pastor as Vocational Counselor. St. Louis: Bethany Press, 1961.

VOCATIONAL GUIDANCE

Brewer, John. History of Vocational Guidance. New York: Harpers, 1942.

Myers, George. Principles and Techniques of Vocational Guidance. New York: McGraw-Hill, 1941.

Sanderson, Herbert. Basic Concepts of Vocational Guidance. New York: McGraw-Hill, 1954.

Williamson, Edmund. Vocational Counseling. New York: McGraw-Hill, 1965.

Some books on Guidance include chapters on vocational guidance. There are many such books; we include only a few.

Hamrin & Paulsen. Counseling Adolescents. Chicago: Science Research Associates, 1950.

Humphreys & Traxler. Guidance Services. Chicago: Science Research Associates, 1954.

Jones, A.J. Principles of Guidance. 6th ed. New York: McGraw-Hill, (1934) 1970.

OCCUPATIONAL INFORMATION

Shartle, Carroll. Occupational Information. Englewood Cliffs, N.J.: Prentice-Hall, 1952.

Baer & Rober. Occupational Information. Chicago: Science Research Associates, 1958.

Hoppack, Robert. Occupational Information. New York: McGraw-Hill, 1957.

Kirk, Barbara. Occupational Information in Counseling. Consulting Psychologists Press, 1964.

TESTING AND VOCATIONAL GUIDANCE

Super, Donald. Appraising Vocational Fitness.

Any text on psychological testing such as those by Cronbach, Goodenough, Freeman, or Ross will include a section on vocational testing.

PSYCHOLOGY OF VOCATIONAL LIFE

Henzberg, Mousner, Snyderman. The Motivation to Work. New York: John Wiley, 1959.

Smith, Henry C. Psychology of Industrial Behavior. 2nd ed. New York: Mc-Graw-Hill, (1955) 1964.

Super, Donald E. Psychology of Careers. New York: Harper & Row, 1957.

RELIGION AND VOCATION

Calhoun, Robert. God and the Day's Work. New York: Association Press, 1946.

Miller, Alexander. Christian Faith and My Job. New York: Association Press, 1943.
Nelson, John. Work and Vocation. New York: Harper & Row, 1954.

Richardson, Alan. The Biblical Doctrine of Work. Naperville, III.: Allenson, 1952.

Trueblood, Elton. Your Other Vocation. New York: Harper & Row, 1952.

The Alcoholic

Every pastor ought to read the "big book" of Alcoholics Anonymous, plus some of their other publications.

Alcoholics Anonymous. New York: Works, 1939.

Alcoholics Anonymous Comes of Age. New York: Harper & Row, 1957.

Twelve Steps and Twelve Traditions. New York: Harper & Row, 1953.

The standard book for the clergyman is:

Clinebell, Howard. Understanding and Counseling the Alcoholic. Rev. ed. Nashville: Abingdon, (1956) 1968.

Another good book is:

Shipp, Tom. Helping the Alcoholic and His Family. Philadelphia: Fortress, 1966.

There are many excellent pamphlets published by Alcoholics Anonymous and the National Council on Alcoholism. All of these are inexpensive; many of them are free. They provide useful information to the pastor, are valuable to put in the hands of others. They are too numerous to be listed here but can be secured from:

General Service Office of Alcoholics Anonymous
305 East 45th Street
New York, New York 10017

National Council on Alcoholism
2 E. 103rd Street
New York, New York 11236

or by contacting the Alcohol Information Center (Council on Alcoholism) in your own community.

Some additional volumes are as follows:

Chafetz and Demone. Alcoholism and Society. New York: Oxford University Press, 1962.

Earle, Clifford. How to Help an Alcoholic. Philadelphia: Westminster, 1952.

Jellinek, Elvin. The Disease Concept of Alcoholism. Hillhouse Press, 1960.

Mann, Marty. Primer on Alcoholism. New York: Holt, Rinehart and Winston, 1958.

Taylor, George. A Sober Faith. New York: Macmillan, 1953.

Chafetz, Morris et al. Frontiers of Alcoholism. New York: Science House, 1970.

Ministry to the Sick

Belgum, David, ed. Religion and Medicine. Ames, Iowa: Iowa State University Press, 1967.

Cabot and Dicks. The Art of Ministering to the Sick. New York: Macmillan, 1936. This was the pioneer volume in this field and has already become a classic.

Sharpe, William. Medicine and the Ministry. New York: Appleton-Century, 1966.

Westberg, Granger. *Minister and Doctor Meet*. New York: Harper & Row, 1961.

White, Dale, ed. *Dialogue in Medicine and Theology*. Nashville: Abingdon, 1967.

Young, Richard. *The Pastor's Hospital Ministry*. Nashville: Broadman Press, 1954.

Young, Richard, and Meiburg, Albert L. *Spiritual Therapy*. New York: Harper & Row, 1960.
Some of the books on psychosomatic medicine (Dunbar, Helen: *Emotions and Bodily Changes*. New York: Columbia University Press, 1954; and Hinsie: *The Person in the Body*, an Introduction to Psychosomatic Medicine) acquaint the pastor with the emotional factors of illness. A book (Van der Berg, J. H. *The Psychology of the Sickbed*, Duquesne University Press, 1966) written for nurses has almost equal application to the pastor.

Ministry to the Sorrowing

Several good studies of the grief problem and the work of the pastor have been published:

Bachmann, Charles. *Ministering to the Grief Sufferers*. Paperback; Philadelphia: Fortress, (1964) 1967.

Fulton, Robert ed. *Death and Identity*. New York: John Wiley & Sons, 1965.

Gatch, Milton. *Death: Meaning and Mortality in Christian Thought and Contemporary Culture*. New York: Seabury, 1969.

Jackson, Edgar. *Understanding Grief*. Nashville: Abingdon, 1957.

————. *The Christian Funeral*. New York: Channel, 1966.

Scherzer, Carl. *Ministering to the Dying*. Englewood Cliffs, N. J.: Prentice-Hall, 1963.

Also some pastoral aid materials have been made available for pastoral use with the sorrowing.

Jackson, Edgar. *For the Living*. New York: Channel, 1963.

———. You and Your Grief. New York: Channel, 1961.

Rogers, William. Ye Shall Be Comforted. Philadelphia: Westminster, 1950.

Westberg, Granger. Good Grief. Rock Island, Ill.: Augustana, 1962.

THE MINISTER AND MENTAL HEALTH

Biddle, William. Integration of Religion and Psychiatry. New York: Macmillan, 1955.

Bruder, Ernest. Ministering to Deeply Troubled People. Englewood Cliffs, N.J.: Prentice-Hall, 1963.

Clinebell, Howard. Mental Health Through Christian Community. Nashville: Abingdon, 1965.

Clinebell, Howard, ed. Community Mental Health. Nashville, Abingdon, 1970.

Fromm, Erich. Psychoanalysis and Religion. New Haven: Yale University Press, 1950.

Hofmann, Hans, ed. The Ministry and Mental Health. New York: Association Press, 1966.

Maves, Paul. The Church and Mental Health. New York: Scribner's, 1953.

McCann, Richard. The Churches and Mental Health. New York: Basic Books, 1962.

Oates, Wayne. Religious Factors in Mental Illness. New York: Association Press, 1955.

FOR THE FAMILY

English, Oliver, and Pearson, Gerald. Emotional Problems of Living. New York: Norton, 1945.

Southard, Samuel. The Family and Mental Illness. Philadelphia: Westminster, 1957.

Stern, Edith. Mental Illness: A Guide for the Family. National Association for Mental Health, The Commonwealth Fund, 1942.

Much valuable material is available in pamphlet form and can be secured from:

The National Association for Mental Health
10 Columbus Circle
New York, New York

or from your local Mental Health Association.

Homosexuality

Cappan, Daniel. Toward a Christian Understanding of Homosexuality. Englewood
Cliffs, N. J.: Prentice-Hall, 1965.

Jones, H. Kimball. Toward a Christian Understanding of the Homosexual. New
York: Association Press, 1966.

Wyden & Wyden. Growing Up Straight. New York: Stein & Day, 1969. (This
is for parents.)

Rehabilitation of Criminal and Delinquent

The literature on crime, delinquency, and criminology is vast in its propor-
tions. The pastor should be familiar with some of it, especially that dealing with
delinquency.

Kandle & Cassler. Ministering to Prisoners and Their Families. Englewood Cliffs,
N.J.: Prentice-Hall, 1968. (This is the one volume prepared specifically
for pastors.)

Some volumes on Crime and Delinquency are:

Aickhorn, August. Delinquency and Child Guidance. New York: International
Universities Press, 1965.

Bloch and Geis. Man, Crime and Society. New York: Random House, 1962.

Cavan, Ruth. Juvenile Delinquency. New York: Lippincott, 1962.

Glueck, Sheldon, and Glueck, Eleanor. Unraveling Juvenile Delinquency. Commonwealth Fund, 1950.

Menninger, Karl. <u>The Crime of Punishment</u>. New York: Viking, 1968.

Tappan, Paul W. <u>Crime, Justice and Correction</u>. New York: McGraw-Hill, 1960.

FOR OBSERVATION AND FURTHER INFORMATION

Visit the local jail and discuss the types of problems that exist in your community with the sheriff or chief of police.

The Church and the Underprivileged

This is another area where the literature is inadequate. Haskell Miller's <u>Compassion and Community</u> (Nashville: Abingdon Press, 1961) was good but is now out of date. The pastor should be familiar with some of the basic texts in social case work and social welfare.

The best single source of information is <u>The Encyclopedia of Social Work</u> published every two years by the National Association of Social Workers. The following are a few of the many studies of poverty in America. They do not discuss pastoral care.

Bagdikian, Ben. <u>In the Midst of Plenty</u>. Signet Book; New York: New American Library, 1964.

Harrington, Michael. <u>The Other America</u>. Baltimore: Penguin Press, 1963.

Leinwand, Gerald. <u>Poverty and the Poor</u>. New York: Washington Square Press, 1968.

Shostak, Arthur, and Gomberg, William, eds. <u>New Perspectives on Poverty</u>. Englewood Cliffs, N.J.: Prentice-Hall, 1965.

The Gifted

The literature on special education or any book on the psychology of the exceptional child usually includes a section on the gifted child.

Abraham, W. <u>Common Sense about Gifted Children</u>. New York: Harper & Row, 1958.

Cox, Catharine M. The Early Mental Traits of Three Hundred Geniuses. Stanford, Calif.: Stanford University Press, 1926.

De Hoon and Havighurst. Educating Gifted Children. Chicago: University of Chicago Press, 1961.

Education of the Gifted. National Education Association, 1950.

Gallagher, James. Teaching the Gifted Child. Boston: Allyn & Bacon, 1964.

Kemp, Charles F. The Church: the Gifted and Retarded Child. St. Louis: Bethany Press, 1957 (the only study of the gifted for the pastor thus far).

Schertzer, B., ed. Working with Superior Students. Chicago: Science Research Associates, 1960.

Terman, Lewis M., and Oden, Melita H. The Gifted Group at Mid Life. Stanford, Calif.: Stanford University Press, 1959.

Terman, Lewis M. et al. The Gifted Child Grows Up. Stanford, Calif.: Stanford University Press, 1947.

Witty, Paul A., ed. The Gifted Child. Lexington, Mass.: Heath, 1951.

Witty, Paul A. Helping the Gifted Child. Chicago: Science Research Associates, 1953.

The Retarded

Any discussion of special education usually includes a section on the retarded. There have been many books on the education, vocational rehabilitation, and counseling with the retarded child. The National Association for Retarded Children publishes many pamphlets, including a bibliography on the church and the retarded. Studies prepared for the pastor are:

Kemp, Charles F. The Church: The Gifted and the Retarded Child. St. Louis: Bethany Press, 1957.

Peterson, Sigmond. Retarded Children: God's Children. Philadelphia: Westminster, 1970.

Stubblefield, Harold. The Church's Ministry in Mental Retardation. Nashville: Broadman, 1965.

The Handicapped

Very little has been written on pastoral counseling with the handicapped. A pastoral aid book to be used with the handicapped is: Wilkie: Strengthened with Might. (Philadelphia: Westminster, 1952). The extensive literature on rehabilitation gives the pastor an understanding of the nature of the handicapped's problems. Any book on special education or the exceptional child will include a section on the handicapped. There are also books which deal with special areas such as speech handicaps, hearing, and usual handicaps, etc.

Older People

Several good books have been written on the church and older people. Some of the better ones are:

Brown, J. Paul. Counseling with Senior Citizens. Englewood Cliffs, N.J.: Prentice-Hall, 1967.

Gray, Robert, and Moburg, David. The Church and the Older Person. Grand Rapids: Eerdmans, 1962.

Maves, Paul, and Cedarleaf, J. Lennart. Older People and the Church. Nashville: Abingdon, 1949.

Also the pastor should be familiar with some of the literature on geriatrics, especially that written by social workers, since their work with the elderly is often very similar to the pastor's. See, for example:

Arthur, Julietta. How to Help Older People. Philadelphia: Lippincott, 1954.

Klein, LeShon, and Furman. Promoting Mental Health of Older People through Group Methods. New York: Manhattan Society for Mental Health, 1967.

The White House Conference on Aging publishes a bibliography of several hundred titles on all aspects of older persons.

Conversion and Religious Growth

All good books on the psychology of religion have a section devoted to conversion. Some of these are quite old but are not without interest.

Clark, Elmer T. The Psychology of Religious Awakening. New York: Macmillan, 1929.

Clark, Walter H. The Psychology of Religion. New York: Macmillan, 1958.

Cutten, George B. Psychological Phenomena of Christianity. New York: Scribner's, 1908.

James, William. Varieties of Religious Experience. London: Longmans, Green & Co., 1917.

Johnson, Paul E. The Psychology of Religion. Rev. ed. Nashville: Abingdon, (1945) 1959.

Mackenzie, John G. Psychology, Psychotherapy and Evangelism. New York: Macmillan, 1940.

Starbuck, Edwin D. The Psychology of Religion. New York: Scribner's, 1901.

Strunk, Orlo. Readings in the Psychology of Religion. Nashville: Abingdon, 1959.

Religious Experience and Religious Problems

Allport, Gordon. The Individual and His Religion. New York: Macmillan, 1950.

Boisen, Anton. Exploration of the Inner World. Chicago: Willett, Clark, 1936.

Clark, Walter. The Psychology of Religion. New York: Macmillan, 1958.

Guntrip, Henry. Psychotherapy and Religion. New York: Macmillan, 1957.

James, William. Varieties of Religious Experience. London: Longmans, Green, 1917.

Johnson, Paul E. The Psychology of Religion. Rev. ed. Nashville: Abingdon, (1945) 1959.

Loomis, Earl. The Self in Pilgrimage. New York: Harper & Row, 1960.

Northridge, William. Disorders of the Emotional and Spiritual Life. London: Epworth, 1960.

Strunk, Orlo. Mature Religion. Nashville: Abingdon, 1965.

Wise, Carroll. Psychiatry and the Bible. New York: Harper & Row, 1958.

Guilt, Confession, and Forgiveness

Countless books have been written on the problems of doubt and faith, guilt and forgiveness, etc. Hardly any have been prepared on counseling persons about such problems. The pastor should be familiar with the concepts of guilt as presented in such books as the following:

Belgum, David. Guilt, Where Religion and Psychiatry Meet. Englewood Cliffs, N. J.: Prentice-Hall, 1963.

Knight, James. Conscience and Guilt. New York: Appleton-Century-Crofts, 1969.

MacKenzie, John G. Guilt: Its Meaning and Significance. Nashville: Abingdon: 1962

Sherrill, Lewis J. Guilt and Redemption. Rev. ed. Richmond: John Knox Press, 1957.

Stein, Edward. Guilt: Theory and Therapy. Philadelphia: Westminster Press, 1968.

Tournier, Paul. Guilt and Grace. London: Hodder & Stoughton, 1962.

Thurian, Max. Confession. London: SCM Press, 1958.

All the books on the psychology of religion from William James's Varieties of Religious Experience (Longmans, Green, 1917) to the more recent studies. The Psychology of Religion by Walter Clark (Macmillan, 1958) and The Psychology of Religious Experience (Longmans, Green, 1917) to the more recent studies. The Psychology of Religion by Walter Clark (Macmillan, 1958) and The Psychology of Religion by Paul Johnson (Abingdon, 1959), discuss such matters as conversion, religion of healthy-mindedness, etc.

Theological Backgrounds of Pastoral Care

Browning, Don. Atonement and Psychotherapy. Philadelphia: Westminster, 1966.

Hiltner, Seward. A Preface to Pastoral Theology. Nashville: Abingdon, 1958.

Howe, Reuel L. Man's Need and God's Action. New York: Seabury, 1954.

Hulme, William E. Counseling and Theology. Philadelphia: Muhlenberg, 1956.

Oates, Wayne E. Christ and Selfhood. New York: Association Press, 1961.

Outler, Albert C. Psychotherapy and the Christian Message. New York: Harper & Row, 1954.

Roberts, David E. Psychotherapy and a Christian View of Man. New York: Scribner's, 1950.

Sherrill, Lewis J. The Gift of Power. New York: Macmillan, 1955.

————. The Struggle of the Soul. New York: Macmillan, 1954.

Thornton, Edward. Theology and Pastoral Counseling. Englewood Cliffs, N.J.: Prentice-Hall, 1964.

Thurneysen, Eduard. A Theology of Pastoral Care. Richmond: John Knox, 1962.

Tillich, Paul. The Courage to Be. New Haven: Yale University Press, 1952.

Williams, Daniel D. The Minister and the Care of Souls. New York: Harper & Row, 1961.

Preaching and Pastoral Care

Most books on Homiletics deal only with the sermon. A very few discuss the people who hear the sermon. A few studies have attempted to show the relationship of preaching and pastoral care. Some are now emphasizing the use of dialogue.

Howe, Reuel. Partners in Preaching. New York: Seabury, 1968.

Jackson, Edgar. Psychology for Preaching. New York: Channel Press, 1961.

Kemp, Charles F. Life-Situation Preaching. St. Louis: Bethany, 1956.

————. Pastoral Preaching. St. Louis: Bethany, 1963.

————. The Preaching Pastor. St. Louis: Bethany, 1966.

Linn, Edmund. Preaching as Counseling, the Unique Method of Harry Emerson Fosdick. Valley Forge, Pa.: Judson, 1966.

Oden, Thomas. Kerygma and Counseling. Philadelphia: Westminster, 1966.

The Pastoral Counselor

Bowers, Margaretta. Conflicts of the Clergy.. Camden, N.J.: Thomas Nelson, 1963.

Hiltner, Seward. The Counselor in Counseling. Nashville: Abingdon, 1952.

Hofmann, Hans, ed. Making the Ministry Relevant. New York: Scribner's, 1960.

Menger, Robert, and Dittes, James. Psychological Studies of Clergymen. Camden, N.J.: Thomas Nelson, 1965.

Niebuhr, H. Richard. The Purpose of the Church and Its Ministry. New York: Harper & Row, 1956.

Niles, Daniel T. The Preacher's Calling: To Be Servant. London: Lutterworth Press, 1959.

Oates, Wayne E. The Minister's Own Mental Health. New York: Channel Press, 1961.

JOURNALS ON PASTORAL CARE

Pastoral Psychology. 400 Community Drive, Manhasset, L.I., N.Y.

Journal of Pastoral Care. The Association for Clinical Pastoral Education, in Cooperation with the American Association of Pastoral Counselors.

The Pastoral Counselor. The American Foundation of Religion and Psychiatry, 3 West 29th, New York, N.Y.

Journal of Religion and Health. National Academy of Religion and Mental Health.

JOURNALS IN RELATED FIELDS

American Journal of Psychiatry. American Psychiatric Association, Baltimore, Md.

American Journal of Psychoanalysis. Association for the Advancement of Psycho-Analysis, New York.

Contemporary Psychology. A journal of reviews. American Psychological Association, Washington, D.C.

Journal of Counseling Psychology, Columbus, Ohio.

Journal of Educational Psychology, Washington, D.C.

Journal of Existential Psychology and Psychiatry. Dubuque, Iowa.

Other journals, such as publications of family counselors, social workers, Association for Retarded Children, etc., may be secured by checking the Reader's Guide or the reference desk in the library.

American Psychologist. American Psychological Association, Lancaster, Pa.

Mental Hygiene Quarterly. National Association of Mental Health, New York.

Personnel and Guidance Journal. American Personnel and Guidance Association, Washington, D.C.

Psychological Review. American Psychological Association, Washington, D.C.